HONDA GOLD WING

SHOEI
Come Ride with Us
Anniversary Edition

HONDA GOLD WING

Malcolm Birkitt

First published in Great Britain in 1995
by Osprey, an imprint of Reed Consumer
Books Limited, Michelin House,
81 Fulham Road, London SW3 6RB and
Auckland, Melbourne, Singapore and Toronto.

ISBN 1 85532 443 1

Project Editor Shaun Barrington
Editor Julia North
Page design Paul Kime/Ward Peacock
Partnership

Printed in Hong Kong

Half title page
Allegiance to the Gold Wing fraternity is often proclaimed by a rider's clothes

Title page
An Anniversary Edition version of the GL1500, made in 1991 to commemorate ten years of Gold Wing production in America, heads a posse of GWOCGB riders

Right
Wings adopt flying formation at a Florida get-together

NLOP K491

Introduction

Honda have a knack for redrawing the motorcycling landscape. Touring on two wheels certainly existed before the Gold Wing, but the introduction of this technological *tour de force* in 1975 forever changed the way people thought about the subject. Here, finally, was a machine which had the power, the refinement, the toting capacity and the looks to draw them away from the American or European bikes they'd known until that point.

By advancing the means of transporting two passengers and their luggage across vast states, or even whole continents, the Gold Wing has, in little more than a generation, become something of an institution. For many, the bike has opened up whole new chapters in the world of motorcycle touring, even attracting those who would not have looked twice at two wheels before.

Gradually increasing its popularity over the years, Honda's flagship tourer has confounded its critics many times, but continually delights its devotees. The Wing is often derided as a two-wheeled car, and indeed the latest versions feature a reverse gear. Yet many American owners would welcome the comparison with the Cadillacs or the Rolls-Royces of this world, as comfort is essential to effective touring. Wings achieve this function with style, pace, smoothness and no small luxury. So, until someone else designs a superior grand touring motorcycle, the Gold Wing will remain the standard by which all other touring motorcycles are judged.

The Gold Wing story is one of continuous refinement of a basic touring concept, sometimes by subtle changes and on at least three occasions by radical revamps of the entire design. The idea may have crystallised in the east, with western consumers in mind, yet it soon became transplanted into its main market. The Gold Wing is now very much an American, not a Japanese, motorcycle. It is built in the USA by Americans for American tastes and sensibilities, and continues to exhibit the style and bulk of American motorcycles. What was once a comparatively simple design now appears to be conspicuously over-engineered, almost elevating complexity to the level of a virtue. The latest version – the GL1500 – is an intricate collection of parts indeed; for example, it carries dozens of electrical relays. Fitting further electrical items – especially non-Honda accessories – is very much done at a rider's own risk!

The Gold Wing's evolution has already spanned two decades of touring excellence, continually remaining true to its central themes of power, smoothness, reliability and comfort. And if the legislators and environmentalists allow, it is to be hoped that the Wing will fly for many a year ahead.

This book is dedicated to Wing nuts everywhere. I have met and photographed countless fans of the Gold Wing while compiling this work, and wish I could meet them all personally again. I'd also like to single out certain individuals for special mentions, including Dave Horner, Secretary of the Gold Wing Owners Club of Great Britain, Sean Warwick and John Noble, editor and chief photographer respectively, of *Motor Cycle News*, Louise Limb for her fine engine illustration, Mick Woollett for library material, and ace photographer Mac McDiarmid for supplementing my own pictures.

Malcolm Birkitt

Right
'So how long does your battery last, then?' American Wing nuts chew the fat alongside an intensively customised GL1200 Aspencade SE-i

Contents

Origins

Soichiro Honda had a vision. His aim was to make the company bearing his name into the world's leading manufacturer of motorcycles. The puny 50cc two-stroke that represented his first machine was, perhaps, an inauspicious start, and few could have predicted what was to follow in the years ahead. The blinkered motorcycling companies of Britain, Europe and America regarded Japanese products with scorn and simply did not perceive them as any kind of threat to the home markets.

The Honda Motor Company was founded in 1948 and, within five years, small capacity four-stroke bikes were rolling off the production line. As the 1950s drew to a close, it became increasingly evident that Honda were becoming a force to be reckoned with; one of their machines finished well up in the 125cc Isle of Man TT races. Small steps became giant strides in the '60s when, for the first time, monthly bike sales topped 100,000 and Honda quickly won the 125cc and 250cc road race world championships.

By 1968, just twenty years on from the first tiny two-strokes, bike production had reached a staggering ten million units, and the two-wheeled world was beginning to sit up and take notice. A year later, the USA and Canada had its first glimpse of the superbike era when exports of the astonishing CB750 four-cylinder machine started. Such was the pace of development kickstarted by Honda, that other Japanese manufacturers such as Yamaha, Suzuki and Kawasaki seemed caught in their slipstream.

As any racing competitor will tell you, this can provide opportunities to pass those ahead, and some reacted quicker than others. Kawasaki temporarily dented Honda's corporate pride by launching a superbike to top the CB750 – the 900cc Z1. Even BMW got in on the act by uprating their venerable boxer twin to the same cubic capacity and adding some sporting pretensions into the mix.

To restore the company's prestige, Soichiro Honda instigated a new project to create the biggest, fastest and best grand touring machine – the King of Motorcycles was the objective. But it wasn't long before the realisation dawned that such a machine couldn't be built, as the criteria demanded by a super-sports machine and an all-out tourer were mutually exclusive. Therefore two diverging design routes were followed, with the sports bike evolving from the successful air-cooled in-line four engine established by the CB750. Ultimately this led to the exotic CBX six-cylinder of 1978, which blew the sports competition away and got everyone checking the small print of the law books to see if such an

Above right
The Gold Wing that never was. Only one AOK prototype was built by Honda in 1972. The motorcycle only weighed 484 lbs and its flat six engine was said to be extremely smooth, but its length prevented a reasonable riding position. The project was called off. Instead, a four-cylinder machine evolved into the Gold Wing

Right
A downdraught two-barrel carburettor fed the AOK's six cylinders, which developed 80 bhp at 6700 rpm. The cradle frame featured engine mountings like those seen on the Honda CB750

HONDA

awesome machine should be prohibited. The 1970s witnessed the biggest ever boom in motorcycling, period. Honda had correctly identified the USA as the largest potential market for their new touring motorcycle – even today, Gold Wing sales are concentrated in North America. So the Japanese began checking out the competition to see how it shaped up. Only one home-grown manufacturer existed, in the shape of Harley-Davidson's mighty Electra Glide. Despite its ancient air-cooled 1200cc V-twin engine, this bike was large, strong and fast enough to carry big American loads over long distances. It had bags of sheer grunt to make up for its inadequacies of performance and lack of nimble handling. But the Harley's engineering qualities left plenty of scope for improvement.

That wasn't a criticism that could be levelled at the other contender on sale in America – the BMW. Though produced in small numbers by Japanese levels, it was built to high standards. Like the Harley, the Germans had created a simple motorcycle with an air-cooled flat twin engine layout that had been refined over several decades. Its main problem was that the vibrations produced by the engine tended to transmit themselves in the form of shudders to the rest of the motorcycle and rider, and significant torque reaction was noticeable during acceleration and braking. Beemers also suffered from a lack of carrying capacity. As Americans tend to tour with an 'everything including the kitchen sink' attitude, the boxer twin's gross weight limit was too readily surpassed.

It was from these disparate references that Honda began to draw their specification for a new touring machine. A high gross weight limit, so that ample gear could be toted, demanded a wide rear tire. To shift all this stuff up hills, a powerful, large-capacity engine was also necessary. Honda decided water-cooling was preferable, to keep things quiet and cool, together with a multi-cylinder layout for a smooth delivery of power. So, by definition, the new Honda had to be smooth, quiet, reliable, shaft-driven and able to carry a large load.

Honda drew up a new set of parameters, encompassing efficiency and greater performance, and their team of brilliant young designers, led by Soichiro Irimajari, set to work in 1972. The motorcycle they produced was the Honda AOK – a remarkable 1470cc horizontally-opposed six-cylinder, weighing a moderate 484 lbs. This single-overhead camshaft design used a bore of 72mm, a stroke of 60mm, had a compression ratio of 8:1 and, breathing through a single carburettor, churned out around 80bhp.

Just one prototype AOK was built, reflecting the influence of several other machines. The cradle frame and engine mountings resembled the CB750, while the shaft drive rear end could have been sawn straight off a BMW. The prototype's engine was reported as delivering plenty of smooth power, and a low centre of gravity gave excellent stability. But the bike

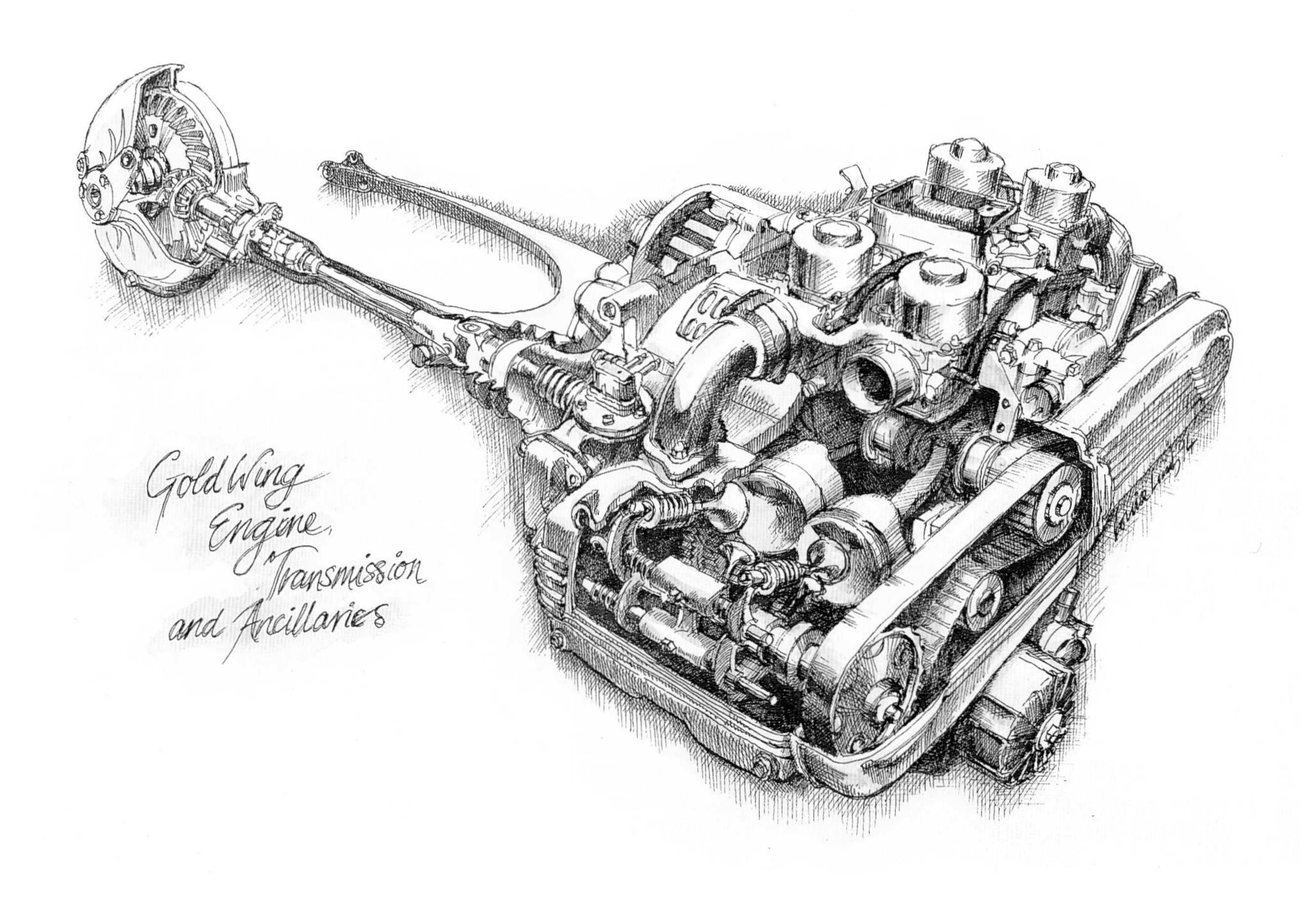

Honda eventually settled on a flat four engine configuration for their grand tourer, with the now familiar toothed-belt driven camshafts at the front of the engine along with the oil filter and water pump. The gearbox was housed beneath the crankshaft in the massive crankcase castings, and the shaft drive fed power to the rear wheel

had one major handicap – though the wheelbase was a reasonable 58.25 inches, the sheer length of the engine meant that a reasonable riding position couldn't be found. So the AOK was yet another motorcycle that failed to make it to production.

Undaunted, Honda installed Toshio Nozue as project leader of the engineering team working on the new tourer, and this time they came up with the goods. A year's intensive development at the company's Tochigi test facility convinced the team they had finally got the bike the company needed to restore its prestige.

First Flight

All the wild speculation in the motorcycling press was finally laid to rest when the first Gold Wing – the K0 model of the GL1000 – was unveiled at the Cologne show in October 1974. Honda had decided to abandon the flat-six motor, and pursue the grand tourer theme with a more compact flat four engine of 999cc capacity. Still water-cooled, this impressive unit employed belt-driven single overhead camshafts, a bank of four 32mm constant-vacuum carburettors, a five-speed gearbox, shaft drive to the rear wheel, and was claimed to weigh 226 lbs dry on its own!

Naturally, a sturdy frame was needed to carry it and Honda opted for a duplex tube design with lots of gussets and welds to enhance stiffness around the rear fork and headstock. Installation of the motor was facilitated by removing the bolted-up bottom left-hand rail of the frame.

The rear fork was integrated with the shaft drive, which carried a universal joint at its front end and a bevel box at the rear. Up front were telescopic forks with hydraulic damping. Spoked wheels were fitted, with a 3.50 x 19 inch tyre on the front and an unusual 4.50 x 17 inch size rubber on the rear. Rumours that this had cost Honda half a million pounds to

Left

The author vividly remembers his first sight of a Honda Gold Wing, at the BMF Rally in 1975. The unfaired 1000cc machine looked gargantuan compared to the other large capacity machines of the day, and carried the same horizontally opposed, water-cooled engine layout that is still the Gold Wing's signature to this day

develop were flatly denied by the manufacturer. Some saw the GL1000 as a revolutionary motorcycle, bristling with new technology. However, few of the features were actually new. Disc brakes, for instance, were now commonplace, but here were three on the same bike for the first time. What the Gold Wing did was bring together in a single motorcycle a whole range of innovations seen on various other models over the years.

Honda had thought of their machine as the first water-cooled bike in production, but the British-made Scott had preceded their efforts by several decades! Other machines had also placed their fuel supply under the seat for a lower centre of gravity. Where the petrol tank was traditionally, the GL1000 had sheet steel, making a dummy shape to cover a host of electrical components and other ancillaries. There were plenty of firsts for a Japanese machine, but the worldwide claims didn't stand up.

Only in one department did the GL1000 break new ground. Mr Nozue had seen that the only real engineering challenge facing him was to overcome the inherent torque reaction of the engine's in-line crankshaft. So he came up with a novel solution, using the AC generator as a contra-rotating flywheel to cancel out these forces.

The GL1000 featured engine dimensions of 72mm x 61.4mm, and had a compression ratio of 9.2:1. Power output at 7500rpm was 80bhp. The wheelbase was 60.5 inches, for optimum straight-line stability, and it weighed a hefty 635 lbs with oil and fuel. The Gold Wing's cylinders were slightly staggered, with the right side ahead of the left as viewed

Above
The 650 lb all-up weight of the GL1000 is well disguised by having the engine slung low in the frame to give a low centre of gravity

Right
A quartet of Keihin 32mm constant velocity carburettors fed the four cylinders of the GL1000

CHOKE
FUEL
GL1000
HONDA

Left

Though a first for many motorcyclists, the fuel gauge in the lid of the dummy tank was both badly positioned, as it got in the way of a tank bag, and hideously inaccurate. Instruments were a pair of dials for the speedometer and tachometer, with a cluster of warning lights between them and an ignition key below. Inset in the speedo were the mileage and trip recorders, while the rev counter area included a temperature gauge

Above

Motorcycle shows put the 1000cc water-cooled flat four GL on a pedestal, to give everyone a good view of Honda's new leader of the road bike range

Above and right
The production version embodied just three minor amendments over the prototype. Changes were made to the radiator cap, a warning sticker was added, and self-cancelling turn signals were omitted

from the riding position, though this was hardly noticeable. Another interesting facet of the flat four was the crankshaft layout, which had the front two pistons moving in opposition to the rear two, to give balance to the primary and secondary forces in the engine, and the primary couples. This left just the insignificant secondary couples.

Honda's publicity supremos of the mid-'70s didn't hold back, and built a lavish promotional campaign around their new creation, even dubbing it 'the ultimate motorcycle'. First reactions in the press were overwhelmingly, if not universally, favourable, with just the odd voice of dissent from the likes of Bill Haylock, then editor of the UK's *Bike* magazine. Here are some of his choicest remarks:

"When is a motorcycle not a motorcycle? No, that's not a cue for any facetious answers – I'm getting seriously worried at the direction the development of Japanese bikes is taking.

"OK, we owe Mr Honda a lot for past services. He and his competitors have done wonders for small cube bikes and made us realise that big roadburners don't have to shake or leak oil. But I have an uneasy feeling that, as far as big bikes are concerned, the Japs are starting to go over the top. They're trying to turn bikers into socially acceptable two wheeled motorists.

"When Honda's Gold Wing became more than just a well-engineered rumour, Honda's publicity machine rumbled into action like a squadron of Chieftan tanks, hoping to conquer the prestige bike market with battle cries like: 'Quite simply the most advanced motorcycle ever made;' 'Acclaimed as the most significant and major achievement in the motorcycle industry for many years;' 'The Ultimate...' Powerful stuff, even to the experienced connoisseurs of public relations bull. Just about everyone did what was required, and obediently gasped in wonder, instead of asking the question, 'The Ultimate what?' "No-one looked too closely at the brash claims, which in actual fact, don't stand too much scrutiny. The flat-four motor is nothing new to motorcycles, nor is water cooling, nor is shaft drive, nor is the dummy tank, nor is the rear disc brake. One of the biggest, fastest, most complex and impressive motor cycles ever made the Gold Wing may be, but the most advanced...?

"In truth, the Gold Wing is a very conventional motorcycle. It is remarkable not so much for technical innovation, as for the change of course it represents, away from traditional motorcycle technology and into line with contemporary automobile technology. It also reflects Honda's avowed policy of making the motorcycle more socially acceptable and safer, even if it also makes them more boring."

After arguing that the GL1000 seemed to be designed with possible future safety legislation in mind, Haylock began to wonder what function the Honda fulfilled. Then it dawned on him that the Wing was an image bike, pure and simple. Complimentary remarks about the smoothness and quietness of the motor, and its outright performance followed, but this was merely the calm before the storm.

Haylock then tore into the Wing's upright riding position, which limited the speed and duration a rider could endure on the unfaired machine. The fuel consumption he also found unrealistic, while the dummy tank housing electrical components came in for some special opprobrium. Then he moved onto the subjects of handling and weight:

"So much for its failings as a motorway cruiser. When you start using the Wing on any other kind of road, rather more fundamental and frightening failings begin to show... the Honda's massive bulk produces peculiar handling traits I've not come across on other bikes. On fast bends it has a tendency to understeer – the inertia of all that weight tries to make the bike continue on a straight line, with the result that the bike takes the bends on a much wider line than you'd intended... At slow speeds, the cornering characteristics are reversed and the bike oversteers... It feels as though the weight is trying to make the bike flop over on its side.

"But the greatest problem of all with the Wing's handling is the massive weight, which is far more than a conventional motorcycle chassis and suspension should have to cope with. I think there is no excuse for a bike to weigh much over 500 lbs, even a sophisticated luxury tourer, and

Right
The reliability and speed of the GL1000 were soon established. In 1976, a Gold Wing ridden by Fred Chase covered the 1530 miles from Cascade, British Columbia to San Luis in Mexico in 18 hours and 25 minutes, averaging 83mph

HONDA
METZELER

ideally it should weigh less... That superfluous hundredweight and a half drags down the performance to the level of a good, light 750, negating the Wing's 250cc advantage, and yet you pay the penalty of higher fuel consumption, poor handling and rapid tyre wear."

The full review in *Bike* contained criticisms Honda UK found either inappropriate or offensive, and led to a lengthy withdrawal of their advertising and test machinery to that publication. Nearly twenty years on, it is easy to see why there was such a fierce controversy. Haylock's thoughtful, well written, wide-ranging but entirely personal viewpoint may not have been the fawning, complimentary piece Honda had anticipated, and perhaps some of his prophetic words were pitched too close to the truth for the corporate giant.

Elsewhere, journalists took the Gold Wing more to their hearts. In America, *Cycle* had a first gawp at the new Wing at a dealer convention

Above
Dressed bikes were in Honda's plans from early on. This Executive version of the GL1000 was built for the UK arm of the company by accessory manufacturers Rickman in 1976, and featured a full fairing, Lester spoked alloy wheels, crash bars, and a rear carrier. Only 52 examples were built

Right
Simple chrome mudguards were still in vogue throughout the 1970s, along with conventional spoked wheels

ONDA
METZELER

in Las Vegas, and assumed it to be 'a soft, posh and mildly-tuned straight-line tourer'. A rapid standing ¼-mile time of 12.92 seconds and terminal speed of over 104mph soon changed their minds. These figures were quick for 1975, and all-important to superbike buyers of the era.

Handling and roadholding qualities – so critical to European riders with lots of twisties to contend with – tended to be less important to American buyers used to long, wide interstates. *Cycle* commented that the Wing didn't ride well over the expansion joints of LA freeways, and found the riding position too cramped for taller pilots. Generally, though, they rated the GL1000 highly, pointing out its excellent reliability and admitting all you had to do apart from stopping for gas was to enjoy the trip.

Sales of the GL1000 in 1975, the year of its launch, ended up achieving a fraction of Honda's targets. Compared to a forecast of 60,000, just 5000 machines hit the streets, with 80% of those American sales. But much of this was due to poor marketing of a new type of machine to a new type of customer, than any grumbles with the bike itself.

A dry weight of 580 lbs, climbing to close to 640 lbs when fully laden with oils and fuel, may have caused riders some initial fears, but the bike was easy to ride once on the move. The weight, much of it slung low to give a decent centre of gravity, meant the GL1000 exhibited the kind of stability the touring set clamoured for.

Above
Fold-out panels were featured on the GL1000's dummy fuel tank – all part of its innovative and car-like image. The centre compartment housed the fuel filler cap with a drain tray, and a tool tray which lifted out to reveal the air cleaner

Above right
Right side cover of the GL1000's dummy tank concealed the radiator header tank, plus an emergency kickstart lever which fitted a jack at the rear of the engine

Right
Electrical components lived behind the left cover of the dummy fuel tank

10A HEAD
5A TAIL
METERLAMP
5A PARKING
5A OIL.TEMP
NEUTRAL
FUEL
15A HORN STOP
TURN

HONDA
JRK643N
GOLDWING
GL1000
HONDA

The GL1000 also exhibited strong straight-line acceleration, and had sufficient power to top 100mph. Few could complain about its meaty performance, yet it could also amble along at 20mph with ease. At 70mph its motor was turning over at a leisurely 4000rpm.

A firm hand on the tiller was needed to negotiate corners, but the first Wing responded well enough without ever falling into anyone's 'sports bike' category. While Harleys liberally let lubrication out, the GL1000 stayed oil-tight. Above all, the Japanese machine was mechanically reliable, putting the home-grown product to shame as they forever needed spannerwork to keep them on the road.

Honda retained a kickstart on the first Gold Wing, though many wondered why they'd bothered. The pedal was actually stored in the toolbox and needed extricating and fitting to the rear of the engine before it could be jumped on. Luckily, few ever needed this emergency measure.

Fuel consumption worked out at around 45-50mpg for those with a light

Above

Few changes were made to the GL1000 for the '76 and '77 model years. This version shows chrome covers for the exhaust header pipes and upper engine brackets, along with extra pinstriping

Left

Triple discs may have looked impressive, but imparted little feel to the rider. At least they slowed the Wing down if plenty of pressure was applied to the controls

touch, while the heaviest throttle hands got anything from 25-30mpg. This highlighted one of the main deficiencies of the first Gold Wing, as the modest four gallon fuel capacity meant frequent 100 mile fill-ups.

Most owners weren't unduly worried about the GL1000's flaws, as a whole aftermarket industry was soon focused on the Gold Wing. You could buy a comfier saddle, a fairing and a whole host of bolt-on goodies and chrome fittings. Honda had experimented with a fairing on the prototype GL1000, and found it quiet, but the first machines in the UK were offered without any form of protection. In America, a top fairing was a Hondaline option from the start, and other fairings were immediately offered by accessory manufacturers such as Vetter to complement the GL1000's fine touring manners. (Realising what revenue was being lost, Honda eventually fitted them to the bike as original equipment in every market.)

Police forces soon realised the potential of the Gold Wing for traffic duties, even though the hard flat seat cannot have been conducive to long days in the saddle

The GL1000 was the first bike from Japan fitted with triple discs

Detachable panniers, often made by Krauser, meant touring aficionados could travel across states and remove them to the motel room if necessary. S&W shocks were often fitted in place of standard items, in attempts to improve handling and suspension.

In the first years of production mainly cosmetic changes were made, with just minor mechanical improvements. The '76 GLs featured a handy grease nipple on the shaft drive, to make lubrication a simple task – some owners of '75 model year bikes thought the shaft drive required nothing doing to it and a few isolated cases of failure were inevitably reported. A slightly comfier seat appeared on the K2 version in 1977, along with tapered roller bearings in the steering head. *Motorcyclist Illustrated* tested the K2 version of the GL1000, and Peter Rae was generally impressed:

"This smooth transition of combustion power into forward motion had made my journey one of the least tiring in my experience. The almost total absence of noise above 50mph also contributed to my comfort, as the water jacketing keeps mechanical sound down to a clicking from the tappets which is soon lost in the breeze. The exhaust too is well silenced, yet emits an authoritative growl when accelerating hard from a standstill. Sitting there with only the wind for accompaniment, my ears free from mechanical assault, body enjoying the complete lack of vibration and my senses revelling in the engine's responsiveness, perhaps you will begin to understand why I just wanted to keep on riding."

With the K3 model of 1978 (KZ in the UK), a styling facelift saw the traditional spoked wheels replaced by ComStars, and another seat, this time with a step in the middle, was fitted. The dummy tank now carried a pod of three instruments on top – fuel gauge, temperature gauge and voltmeter. More importantly, some much-needed changes were introduced to the motor.

Along with smaller diameter 31mm Keihin carburettors, a radical change of valve timing and more ignition advance saw the 999cc engine produce a flatter power curve. This produced a slightly lower maximum output of 78bhp, but improved mid-range performance, as maximum torque was now at just over 5500rpm instead of 1000rpm higher.

Gear ratios were left unchanged, but riders soon noticed that the K3 had better overtaking ability, and needed less downshifting on gradients. The trade-off was a fractionally slower maximum of 120mph, and a reduced standing ¼-mile time of 13.4 seconds. Most commented that they preferred mid-range grunt to out-and-out top speed anyway.

Suspension was the department that Wing riders liked least. The machine's high weight necessitated stiff springing and damping, which worked well on smooth surfaces, but became choppy on imperfect roads. Loading the bike up with lots of extras didn't help matters either. Many tried accessory units but these stiffer set-ups, which avoided fork bottoming when fully laden, didn't deliver as good a ride quality when the bike was ridden solo.

Late in the '70s, stricter emission regulations in the USA were beginning to have their effect, causing the K3 Wing to be cold-blooded in character. It warmed up reluctantly from cold, then ran with annoying flat spots once it had reached normal running temperatures. Other manufacturers hadn't been idle either, with the new-for-1978 Yamaha XS1100 heading the three year old Wing as the best long-distance bike.

Because motorcycle technology was improving, machines from various manufacturers were now ahead of the Gold Wing, simply because they were designed later. In a six machine comparison in June 1979, the American magazine *Motorcyclist* rated the GL1000 a loser on the grounds of poor ride comfort, excessive weight, poor handling, poor throttle response and peaky powerband.

Though approaching eighty years of age, Tommy Potter still rides two Wings – a GL1200 in Majorca where he lives, and an immaculate GL1000 when back in Britain seeing his family. Here he talks to Dave Horner, Secretary of the Gold Wing Owners' Club of Great Britain at a 'Wing Ding'

One of the first GL1000 press bikes on test in Britain. Opinion was mostly favourable but one magazine's dissenting voice created quite a stir

Despite falling behind in the race for technical progress within the motorcycle industry, the GL1000 continued to sell strongly in the USA and, since being launched, almost a quarter of a million machines had been registered. Uncomplimentary press reviews did not have a catastrophic effect upon the bike's popularity, because many riders prefer to make up their own minds. They are usually more concerned about how a machine feels out on the highway than the reflections of professional journalists. However, it was clearly time for Honda to pay serious attention to their big tourer.

HONDA
GOLDWING
GL1000
METZELER
MICHELIN

Left

Back in 1975, the GL1000 was considered to be a heavyweight motorcycle. Twenty years on, the GL1500 is 25% heavier!

Above

The first big change to the GL1000 came in 1978 with the revamped K3 model, known as the KZ in Europe. It included a list of minor engine mods, a change of rear suspension (but with no noticeable improvement in handling), and stylish Comstar wheels

Above
An all-chrome exhaust system featured on the GL1000 KZ, along with an instrument pod on top of the dummy fuel tank. European riders often fitted a tank bag to obscure them, and the inaccurate fuel gauge was useless anyway

Right
Dad takes junior for a spin along Daytona Beach on his much-modded GL1000 K3

BATES

Above

This beautifully customised 1977 GL1000 typifies the money and care many Wing owners lavish on their machines

Right

Harrogate in Yorkshire, England comes to a halt as the Gold Wing Owners' Club of Great Britain hold their procession

Wing Expands

Although the first Gold Wing had been a great bike, some of its shortcomings had come to light in the latter half of the 1970s as the two-wheel touring fraternity became more demanding and sophisticated. The GL1000 was truculent when cold, had power characteristics which were not ideally suited to touring, poor suspension and seating and meagre load capacity. It was just about tolerable as a tourer, and the competition had now caught up.

Therefore, it came as no surprise when Honda wheeled out a vastly improved machine in 1980. Naturally, the basic mechanical layout and appearance remained similar, with a water-cooled flat-four mill transmitting its power by shaft drive to the rear wheel. Honda were keen to retain those qualities that had already endeared the Gold Wing to nearly a quarter of a million owners. Yet engine displacement was increased by 86cc to 1085cc, aiding the renewed marketing effort as well as boosting mid-range power.

These improvements could have been anticipated, so perhaps the most surprising thing about the GL1100 was where it was built. Honda had first established a motorcycle manufacturing facility at Marysville, Ohio in March 1978, and the plant opened in 1979 with a production capacity of 60,000 units. Most parts still came from Japan, and the new Gold Wing GL1100 – actually Honda's third US-built bike – began rolling off the production line in 1980.

At one time such a notion would have been extremely politically sensitive, but as the 1980s dawned it hardly seemed an issue. Suddenly the Japanese were building motorcycles in America's own back yard and, some said, doing it a sight better than the last vestige of their home industry, Harley-Davidson.

Project leader for the revamped tourer was Shuji Tanaka, an experienced frame designer who took over in 1979. Extra displacement was gained by increasing the bore by 3mm up to 75mm. There were also many other refinements inside the engine. A new, tougher crankshaft was incorporated, even though the previous design had seemed well up to the job, with just a few failures in Europe marring an otherwise impeccable reliability record. Longer valve durations and revised carburation, with yet smaller 30mm Keihin CVs, were also witnessed, all designed to enhance the GL1100's low and mid-range output.

On the ignition front, Honda jettisoned the mechanical contact breaker

Honda's efforts to improve the Wing and see off increasing competition led to the GL1100 of 1980. Apart from the larger engine displacement, the biggest changes were to the seat and suspension. Note also the shapely, valanced mudguards

points, and fitted a magnetic triggering system at the rear of the motor. A simple vacuum advance mechanism, similar to automotive practice, was also included to marry the ignition advance to the engine load. The clutch was wholly new, with plates 7mm larger than before, and a stronger gearbox output shaft was fitted.

Breathing on the 1100cc engine gave an approximate 10% increase in horsepower and much stronger mid-range urge. The new Gold Wing blasted through the ¼-mile in 12.5 seconds with a terminal speed of over 107mph, making it nearly a whole second faster than the GL1000. These excellent figures were certainly due to higher power, but also to lower weight – the GL1100 tipped the scales at 637 lbs wet, down 13 lbs.

The new Wing stretched an already ample 60.8 inch wheelbase out to an astonishing 63.2 inches which, coupled with its 'slow' steering geometry, gave exceptional straight-line stability. The extra length came

from a 1.2 inch longer frame and elongated swinging arm members. Tubeless tires were fitted, and the disturbing high-speed weaves that some riders had experienced on later GL1000s were now a thing of the past.

In answer to widely-voiced criticism of the Wing's suspension, a wholly new air-assisted set-up was introduced. Thicker 39mm front forks containing conventional coil springs gave 5.6 inches of travel, but most of the support was provided by air pressure. A single valve on top of the right-hand stanchion permitted air to be added or bled off, with the pressure checked by a gauge included in the tool kit. Anti-stiction bearings inserts were also incorporated in each fork to reduce sliding friction and make the whole assembly more responsive.

Honda recommended the use of between 14 and 21 pounds per square inch in the front forks, with the higher setting for when the machine was heavily loaded. At 21 psi, surface irregularities could be felt through the

Accessory manufacturers immediately rose to the challenge of the GL1100. Motad equipped their Honda with front fork gaiters, engine protection bars, a replacement exhaust system and chrome rear rack

Most Gold Wing owners had dressed their bikes since its debut in 1975, and it took Honda five years to belatedly offer their own fully kitted-out production machine. Labelled the Interstate (or DX-B in Britain), it is a name that has echoed regularly in the range since. The detachable top box and fixed panniers were standard in the US, but extra cost options in the UK

stiffer fork but the ride was streets ahead of the previous system.

Air shocks were also fitted at the rear, giving almost 4.5 inches of suspension travel. Each unit was half-filled with oil, and had a pressure range of 28 to 43 psi. Higher air pressures meant oil flowed from the reservoir into a secondary volume at a slower rate, giving a nicely progressive set-up. The two rear units were again linked, with the air valve tucked behind the right-side cover, where it made taking readings slightly awkward. At minimum pressure the Wing gave a serene ride quality, while higher figures were still comfortable and had the added benefit of raising ground clearance slightly.

Further comfort was found in the luxurious new seat, which adopted a 'king-and-queen' custom look. Set slightly lower than before, it had a distinct two-inch step between its fore and aft sections, and could be adjusted to and fro by about an inch-and-a-half. A bit of work with an

Left
The 1981 Interstate featured no fewer than twelve locks across the motorcycle. Engine protection bars were a good idea but they extended too far back and were responsible for many a bruised shin. A short shield was placed over the instruments to prevent unwanted reflections in the screen during night riding

Right
The GL1100's frame-mounted fairing meant the headlamp pointed straight ahead regardless of where the handlebars were turned. Air scoops with adjustable vents were also included in the fairing

Allen key was all it took to locate the preferred riding position.

Much attention had, therefore, been paid to the mechanical and dynamic qualities of Honda's new tourer; nor had its appearance been neglected. Changes were seen right from the tip of the front fender – now a stylish, shapely, valanced plastic unit – to the huge twin-bulb rear lights. All-black ComStar wheels, with fatter rims, featured; as well as distinctive polished alloy rocker box covers. However, the most significant change was left for the dummy fuel tank.

The fold-down door design of the first Wing's unit was jettisoned, partly because it was felt to be somewhat 'gimmicky', and because Honda was about to introduce accessory fairings for its replacement. A two-piece lid, with the flaps independently accessible, replaced it. The lower one uncovered the gas cap, meaning that stuff mounted on the tank didn't have to be disturbed. A small fifth-of-a-gallon increase in fuel capacity extended the Wing's touring range a tad.

All these factors made the GL1100 a much more civilised bike to ride. The extra urge of the motor and the newly compliant suspension were the most noticeable transformations. New, powerful discs all round gave strong and predictable stopping power and even the fuel gauge, previously a hopeless device, had pretensions towards accuracy.

In May 1980, *Cycle World* ran a six bike comparison of touring machines, fielding almost exactly the same line-up as tested by *Motorcyclist* just under a year before. This time the revised GL1100 came out top of the reckonings, with an absolutely trouble-free nature. The

HONDA
HONDA
HONDA

HONDA
HONDA

Left

A 1982 GL1100 DX (Interstate) on test for a British motorcycling publication of the era. Despite weighing an extra 100 lbs over the plain version, it was priced attractively and became an instant success in all its markets

Above

The extra urge of the GL1100 engine was well suited to sidecar use, though this conversion to leading link suspension would score few points in a beauty contest!

HONDA
HONDA

Left

Excellent protection for the rider was afforded by the Interstate's full fairing. At last Honda had jumped on the dresser bandwagon

Above

Take one Plain Jane GL1100, add an owner with a little imagination and a healthy wallet, and this is what you get. Honda's own dresser exhibited a little more sobriety when it appeared in late 1980

Above

Somewhere underneath all those chrome accessories and fancy paint lurks a standard GL1100 Interstate. At a standstill it's a picture, while floorboards and backrests for both rider and passenger increase the comfort zone on the move

Right

A GL1100 Interstate out of the crate and gassed up weighed 739 lbs, but your guess is as good as mine as to what this one sits on the scales at. Even the scoop cover for the oil filter is chromed

Overleaf

Happy days on the Interstate, in every sense

HONDA
HONDA
GoldWing

HONDA

Wing had regained the touring crown, but even more was in store for the 1980 model year.

Ever since the first Wing had hit the streets, around 80% of owners had decided to add a fairing to the machine. A thriving aftermarket supply of fairings, saddlebags and radios had sprung up to support the bare GL1000, and the same companies were looking forward to equipping owners of the new tourer. But Honda had plans of their own.

Later that year, a GL1100 Interstate (DX in the UK) was announced; this was offered as a fully-equipped touring package. It boasted a frame-mounted fairing with lowers, a windshield with an inch height adjustment, permanently attached 36-litre panniers with lightweight travel bags inside, a removable 49-litre top box big enough to swallow two full-face helmets and a set of engine protection bars. Each was beautifully integrated into the Wing and perfectly colour matched too, giving the bike

1982 saw the launch of the GL1100 Aspencade, with even more luxury features than the Interstate. Pampering its owner with extras, the Aspencade had an on-board air-compressor for suspension adjustments, a standard stereo and that essential item for the image bike – a vanity mirror in the lid of the travel trunk. Two-tone paint differentiated it from lesser machines a whole new unity of appearance. Further options included a stereo radio, cassette deck, intercom for rider/passenger and a 2-inch taller screen.

With its touring extras, the Interstate weighed 103 lbs more than the bare bike at 739 lbs. Bearing in mind the gross vehicle weight rating of 1105 lbs reduced its load carrying capacity to 366 lbs. The paying public loved it and Honda sold every machine they could churn out. At one point, Honda considered dropping the plain version from the range, but changed their minds when the outcry from the accessory manufacturers became deafening.

There was little sensation of speed when driving the Interstate, as the fairing cocooned the rider and hid the adjacent tarmac slipping under the wheels. The quietness of the engine also had something to do with its uncannily tranquil forward progress. Only taller riders felt a little buffeting of their helmets by turbulent air passing over the screen.

Highway stability was assured, due to Honda's carefully designed steering, frame geometry and weight distribution. A 6 lb iron weight was added between the front fork tubes, to add mass to the steering assembly and make it less prone to weaving at speed. More care was required at trundling speeds, as there was extra weight to contend with. And just about everyone banged their shins on those darned engine safety bars.

Other faults were few and far between. Riders still criticised the seat, however, so this was subtly modified in 1981, becoming lower, softer and with contours more in tune with the American butt! You could also alter its position without delving into the tool kit. Other changes for that year included an increase in maximum air pressure for the rear suspension, self-cancelling indicators similar to those seen on the pre-production GL1000, a new scratch-resistant windshield and a switch to US Dunlop tyres.

For 1982, the basic Wing and Interstate received more minor modifications, such as dual-piston brake calipers, new passenger footrests to reduce vibration (what vibration, we wondered?), revised engine bars, lower ratios for the top three gears and wider tyres. The latter were fitted to smaller ComStar wheels – 18 inch up front and a chunky 16-incher at the rear, said to last a useful 15,000 miles. More rubber on the road helped to up the gross vehicle weight by 25 lbs. Redesigned saddlebag lids, to prevent water penetration, also featured on the faired model.

The real news for 1982 was the debut of the GL1100 Aspencade – an even more luxurious version of the Gold Wing. Here, Honda blitzed the opposition by offering for sale the most fully-equipped and thoughtfully detailed touring motorcycle ever. For techno fans, the air suspension was operated by push-buttons on a console, though it could only be adjusted at a standstill with the ignition key in the 'Park' position, so changes couldn't be attempted on the move. The A-bike sported ventilated discs, and its

HONDA
GOLDWING
Aspencade
MICHELIN

Left

This GL1100 owner's eyes must have lit up when he first spotted the colour of this official Gold Wing jacket

Above

One of the prettiest GL1100 Aspencades I've come across was found at a GWOCGB rally in Somerset. This 1983 example, owned by Richard Dan from Penzance, had the familiar ComStar wheels fitted to UK versions. During the 70,000 miles he's covered on the machine in almost ten years, only one problem has ever arisen – a blown head gasket

Left
In the UK, Honda's 1983 motorcycle brochure made big noises about the GL1100 Aspencade's new digital LCD instrument display

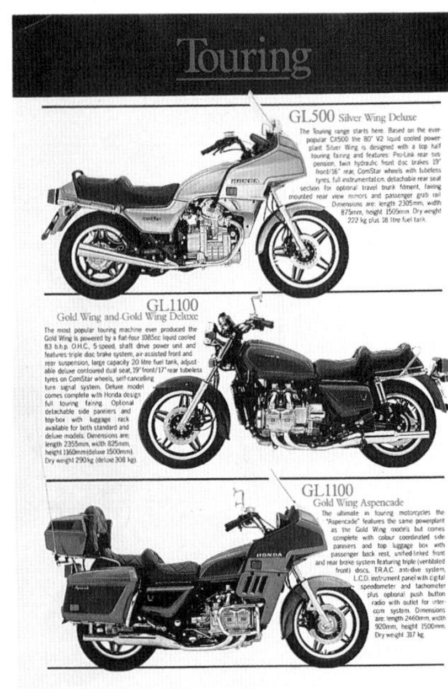

Touring

GL500 Silver Wing Deluxe

The Touring range starts here. Based on the ever-popular CX500 the 80° V2 liquid cooled power-plant Silver Wing is designed with a top half touring fairing and features: Pro-Link rear suspension, twin hydraulic front disc brakes 19" front/16" rear, ComStar wheels with tubeless tyres, full instrumentation, detachable rear seat section for optional travel trunk fitment, fairing mounted rear view mirrors and passenger grab rail. Dimensions are: length 2305mm, width 875mm, height 1505mm. Dry weight 222 kg plus 18 litre fuel tank.

GL1100
Gold Wing and Gold Wing Deluxe

The most popular touring machine ever produced the Gold Wing is powered by a flat-four 1085cc liquid cooled 83 b.h.p. O.H.C., 5-speed, shaft drive power unit and features: triple disc brake system, air-assisted front and rear suspension, large capacity 20 litre fuel tank, adjustable deluxe contoured dual seat, 19" front/17" rear tubeless tyres on ComStar wheels, self-canceling turn signal system. Deluxe model comes complete with Honda design full touring fairing. Optional detachable side panniers and top-box with luggage rack available for both standard and deluxe models. Dimensions are: length 2355mm, width 825mm, height 1160mm (deluxe 1500mm). Dry weight 290 kg (deluxe 308 kg).

GL1100
Gold Wing Aspencade

The ultimate in touring motorcycles the "Aspencade" features the same powerplant as the Gold Wing models but comes complete with colour coordinated side panniers and top luggage box with passenger back rest, unified-linked front and rear brake system featuring triple (ventilated front) discs, T.R.A.C. anti-dive system, L.C.D. instrument panel with digital speedometer and tachometer plus optional push button radio with outlet for inter-com system. Dimensions are: length 2460mm, width 920mm, height 1500mm. Dry weight 317 kg.

Above
Honda's Wing line-up for '83 comprised three Golds and a Silver. The unfaired machine soldiered on, but the dressed Interstate and Aspencade versions were far more popular. A 500cc Silver Wing was a lower budget, middleweight version of its bigger brothers

kerb weight climbed to 766 lbs, so the race to the ¼-mile post had softened to 13.5 seconds.

Handsomely finished in striking two-tone paint schemes, here was the ultimate two-wheeler for serious travellers. Fingertip control of the standard-fit stereo was a neat refinement for the increasing band of riders who liked to sail down the highway accompanied by music. Another new seat was fitted with a new backrest, with a zipped pouch on each side.

Fuel consumption on an Aspencade, with two people aboard plus lots of luggage, depended on the conditions. Drifting effortlessly down highways gave around 45mpg, but this could dip to the mid-30s if full performance was exploited in hillier areas. Solo riders who observed national speed limits would probably get nearly 50mpg, but take oceans of time going places. Typically, the bike would cover about 180 miles before the reserve supply was required.

After all this frenetic activity, most assumed that Honda would add only cosmetic touches to the GL1100, but the '83 models were considerably modified. A major change came in instrumentation, with the all-new LCD bar graphs and digital displays – a refreshing way of gathering, processing and presenting information to the rider. Four LCD windows showed speed, rpm, engine coolant temperature, fuel level, gear selection and suspension air pressure on a high-resolution green background.

A gadget lover's playground; you could program certain data into the system, so it could tell you the miles you'd covered and how many more there were to go to your destination! There was even a maintenance

Above
American versions of the GL1100 Aspencade sported cast wheels for 1983, and abbreviated engine bars to stop riders bashing their shins. Unpredictable March weather meant this Florida gathering of Wings saw plenty of mopping up before bikes were returned to their pristine condition

indicator, which changed colour at 8,000 mile intervals to advise of oil and filter changes. This remarkable method of LCD communication suddenly seemed light years away from the pair of instruments traditional motorcyclists were accustomed to.

Other innovations for 1983 included the fitting of an adjustable TRAC anti-dive system, which used front brake torque reaction to instigate fork resistance, and a unified braking system. Foot pressure on the brake pedal activated the rear disc, naturally, and the right front brake too, while the handlebar lever operated just the left disc up front. A clever pressure control valve meant rear wheel lock-ups were less likely.

The entire range now featured 11-spoke cast alloy wheels, a removable fender section to enable the rear wheel to be taken out more easily, a box-section swinging arm, and details like flatter footrests and a new front fork brace. There were further changes to the seat, and the full dress tourers had their travel trunks moved back and higher to enhance passenger comfort.

Subsequent modifications to the bike's suspension saw the springs in the front forks stiffened and greater damping introduced. The rear shocks were stiffened too, and relied more on the coil spring than air. These machines could even run without air in the suspension. On the Aspencade, the small on-board compressor now worked when the ignition key was at the 'on' position, and the buttons for air control shifted from the tank top up on top of the forks.

Taller gearing led to lower revs and more relaxed cruising on the '83 GL1100s, but had a detrimental effect on acceleration. It meant that the bigger-engined Honda needed to be downshifted more often for safe overtaking or blasts up hills – something Wing fans thought they'd seen disappear with the old 1000cc model.

Opposite

Comings and goings in the Somerset countryside; sweeping through bends in a convoy, members of the Gold Wing Riders' Club of Great Britain let their Wings unfurl. The 1100 wasn't the end of the Gold Wing story of course: the Anniversary Edition GL1500 (below) would appear in 1991

C918
VBY

SHOEI

New Wing, Old Clothes

Just as the heat of competition – in the form of Yamaha's XS1100 – had forced Honda's hand towards the end of the '70s, other machines were making headway in the touring market in the early '80s. BMW's lightweight and fully-faired R100RT had carved itself a niche, and 1100cc in-line fours from Suzuki, Kawasaki and Yamaha, each decked out with touring accessories, were also nibbling away at Gold Wing territory.

Then in 1983 another principal rival, again wearing a Yamaha badge, upped the ante. The XVZ1200 Venture was launched, and quickly became regarded as a superbly integrated touring package. Here was a design of considerable merit that made serious assault on the Gold Wing's touring supremacy. The advanced V-four Yamaha sported a bigger cube motor than the GL1100, leaving it for dead in performance terms, handled well and, with its 'swoopy' bodywork, looked extremely handsome too.

Other manufacturers were hardly idle as 1984 approached. Kawasaki built a touring machine – labelled the Voyager – around their vast 1300cc in-line six, making it the largest and most elaborately outfitted production motorcycle in history. Even that slumbering giant Harley-Davidson showed signs of emerging from the doldrums, by re-engineering their perennial V-twin. Powered by the 1340cc Evolution motor, the Tour Glide was beginning to enter the reckoning too.

The challenge had been well and truly thrown down, and the response from Honda was almost immediate. Shuji Tanaka was still in charge of the design team and, in early 1984, the GL1200 Gold Wing was announced. Vehicle manufacturers often employ sleight of hand to make a so-called 'new' model seem newer than it really is. A couple of minor engineering mods, the reshaping of one or two bits of bodywork and a lick of fresh paint, all held together with a few outlandish claims, sometimes constitutes a new model. In reality, though, it's the same old thing underneath.

But not Honda. They took exactly the opposite route. Everything about the bike was new, from the ground up: engine, frame, wheels, fairing, luggage, seat, suspension, the lot. Yet the newcomer didn't look vastly different to the GL1100 it had replaced. Why? Honda wanted to avoid alienating loyal Gold Wing aficionados, who knew the essence of the bike and didn't wish to move away from this.

Like Yamaha, Honda could have taken a different course, as they had also been developing a V-four engine for road machines. This could have

Subtle external changes were seen on the new GL1200 in 1984. The whole machine had actually been carefully redesigned and improved, but the stylists ensured its lines and proportions were similar to what had been before. The travel trunk was now even roomier and non-detachable

HONDA
HONDA
DUNLOP

HONDA
1200
GOLDWING

been the centrepiece of an exciting new avenue for the Gold Wing, but too much was at stake and the designers remained loyal to the liquid-cooled, horizontally-opposed configuration with belt-driven overhead cams. The new tourer was radically different to what had gone before, yet at the same time appeared conservative in its changes – a neat trick to improve Honda's touring institution.

The GL1200 featured an all-new powerplant, yet bore a strong superficial resemblance to the previous 1085cc unit. Only the fuel and oil pumps carried over from the GL1100. Capacity was enlarged up to 1182cc by lengthening the stroke from 61.4 to 66mm, and by opening up the bore a tad, to 75.5mm.

A quartet of 32mm Keihin CV carburettors squirted fuel through larger 36mm inlet valves into a combustion chamber with a more efficient cylinder head design. Modified valve timing with longer valve lift duration and computerised ignition also contributed to an increased output

Above
Honda retained the LCD instruments on the Aspencade, but rationalised the design further. A taller windshield gave better protection. UK-spec models featured mirrors on the handlebars

Left
Bruised and bashed shins were a thing of the past when Honda's redesigned GL1200 moved its engine further forward in the frame

of 94bhp at 7000rpm. Maximum torque was produced at a lower 5000rpm peak, and the engine's redline was now 7500rpm.

An entirely redesigned chassis wrapped around this mill. Smaller wheels and tyres, with a nine-spoke 16-inch cast alloy at the front and a matching 15-incher at the rear, were fitted to lower the overall centre of gravity and provide quicker steering. Wider tyres also meant the swinging arm fork was 5mm broader. The nose of the engine was angled up 3° from the horizontal, and the whole unit placed 2.5 inches further forward to shift the balance more towards the front wheel, thus making the Wing a better two-up proposition. Improved handling was also sought by dragging back and lowering the steering head, and revising steering geometry with more rake and less trail. The swinging arm was lengthened by over 2 inches, but the wheelbase grew just ⅕ of an inch to 63.4 inches.

Above

Though other Hondas had successfully converted to single-shock rear suspension, the Wing carried on with a conventional dual spring layout. With the transmission under the crankcases, there was little room for this type of suspension layout

Right

Unfaired machines continued in the range until 1985. This neatly customised 'bare' GL1200 gives a better view of the new, smaller and lighter two-section radiator, which had greater airflow and more cooling. An electric cooling fan kicks in as and when required

HONDA
1200
MICHELIN
HI-TOUR A67

Above
Like previous Wings, cornering clearance on the GL1200 was strictly limited. Enthusiastic riding soon had the footrests grounding, so it was best to ride at a leisurely touring pace

Right
GL1200 Aspencade owners now had a roomier glove box in the dummy fuel tank, as the on-board compressor was relocated to the right side of the fairing. An outlet valve and six foot air hose was also supplied – useful for inflating tyres or air mattresses. Bits and bobs could be stored in compartments on either side of the fairing, one of which was lockable

AIR PRESSURE CONTROL
FRONT
INCREASE
AIR PRESSURE
REAR
DECREASE
COMPRESSOR AIR OUTLET
OUTLET VALVE
PUSH ON
CAUTION
HONDA
GOLDWING

HONDA
HONDA
GOLDWING
1200

The final moves to help the new GL cope with twistier sections of tarmac came in the shape of a stiffer front fork, with a pair of beefy 41mm diameter tubes, still wearing the TRAC anti-dive system. Other machines in the Honda range sported the Pro-Link single shock rear end, but two conventionally placed legs remained on the Wing in order not to pinch space from the under-seat fuel tank. Stiffer springs and lower compression damping at both ends, together with stronger rebound damping for the rear shocks, were also apparent.

While the 'Plain Jane' unfaired version of the GL1200 tipped the scales at a modest 665 lbs, the Aspencade crushed them at 790 lbs when fully fuelled. Yet both were far more agile motorcycles than their previous 1100cc counterparts. Any performance advantage, however, was wiped out by the increases in weight and still taller gearing. A typical figure for the standing ¼-mile was a little over 13 seconds; although the GL1200 had considerably more power, it was no faster than previous Wings.

Daily life with the GL1200 was easier too. Its maintenance was

Above

A standard fit on GL1200 Aspencades from the 1984 launch were floorboards for passengers

Left

Aspencades and Interstates for the USA had fairing-mounted mirrors which helped protect a rider's hands from wind buffeting

HONDA

Left
If the GL1200's 25% extra carrying capacity still didn't satisfy, a chrome rack on the travel trunk was a popular accessory

Above
To avoid backache, many riders fitted an aftermarket backrest. It folds down out of the way to allow the passenger to climb aboard

simplified by the incorporation of hydraulic tappets, which needed no adjustment, and hydraulic clutch operation which automatically took up any wear. True to the Gold Wing tradition, you just turned the key and went. Honda were well aware that Gold Wing riders liked to bolt on extra electrical knick-knacks, so the alternator's output was uprated by 20% to 360 watts.

Visually, the new fairing may have carried many echoes of its GL1100 ancestry, but was also entirely new and more efficient at keeping the elements at bay. A taller screen and mirrors fitted to the fairing's sides deflected the breeze away from most riders' heads and hands. This reduced buffeting and wind noise, but let you hear a little more of the motorcycle's innards spinning around – the typical Wing whine owners came to know and live with.

Simplified instrumentation in the fairing, still mainly via LCD displays

Above
Breezing along the highway with the stereo pumping out – is there a better mode of two-wheeled travel than the Wing? For a certain breed of rider, the answer is no

Right
Extra engine panelling on this GL1200 provides an even broader canvas for the custom paint treatment

1200

on the Aspencade, helped a rider assimilate information faster. The rev counter, however, was now digital only and did not show a redline, so throttle happy pilots could approach the 7500rpm limit without knowing it. To prevent this, a warning light flashed when the engine reached 6500rpm, and remained illuminated at 7500rpm. The only mechanical instrument in the cluster was the odometer.

Load capacity had now increased to 380 lbs, so the luggage sections of the GL now swallowed 25% more stuff than the '83 Interstate or Aspencade. O-ring waterproof gaskets on the saddlebags and travel trunk kept it all dry. The seat was another redesigned item, with a wider rear portion and backrest, plus a narrower splay for the passenger's legs. It could be adjusted to any of three positions and was extremely comfortable too. Passengers now had small footboards to rest their feet on, and these folded up out of the way when not in use.

Above
Customising your Gold Wing is all a matter of personal taste – one person's pride and joy is another's nightmare. Personally, I would find the seating compartment on this GL1200 Interstate a little hard to stomach in the mornings!

Right
Eagles are a popular custom paint theme, and owners seem to compete to see who can cram the most lights onto their machines

INTERSTATE
JUL
FLORIDA
92
304040

One of Honda's main aims for the GL1200 – to increase output at low revs – appeared to have been achieved, because the new bike felt more tractable. The bigger motor was still a most civilised and quiet unit; its smoothness tempted some owners to blip the throttle now and again just to make sure it hadn't fallen out! In top gear at 60mph, the bike simply loafed along at just under 3000rpm. The smaller wheels and lower centre of gravity also created the impression that this new Wing was more compact, smaller and lighter than it really was.

On the road, the Honda had a new tautness about its ride quality, transmitting more feel to the rider and a greater sense of confidence. The GL felt light and flicked from side to side with ease. There was none of the top-heaviness apparent with the Yamaha Venture, nor did it seem to be occasionally defying the laws of physics like the comprehensively-equipped but dynamically challenged 1300cc Kawasaki. Limited cornering

Above
1985 saw the marketing men gain the upper hand at Honda, with the launch of a Special Edition version of the Aspencade. Fuel injection and a few extra gizmos gave the bike a certain exclusivity, but at a hefty premium

Right
A GL1200 leads an 1100 and a six-cylinder 1500 on a run out for members of the Gold Wing Owners' Club of Great Britain. You win a prize if you find two bikes that look alike

SHOEI

Left and right
Honda's brochure for the 1986 Gold Wing concentrated on its technological approach to touring. The Interstate was now the cooking model, followed by the Aspencade and the Aspencade SE-i at the top of the range

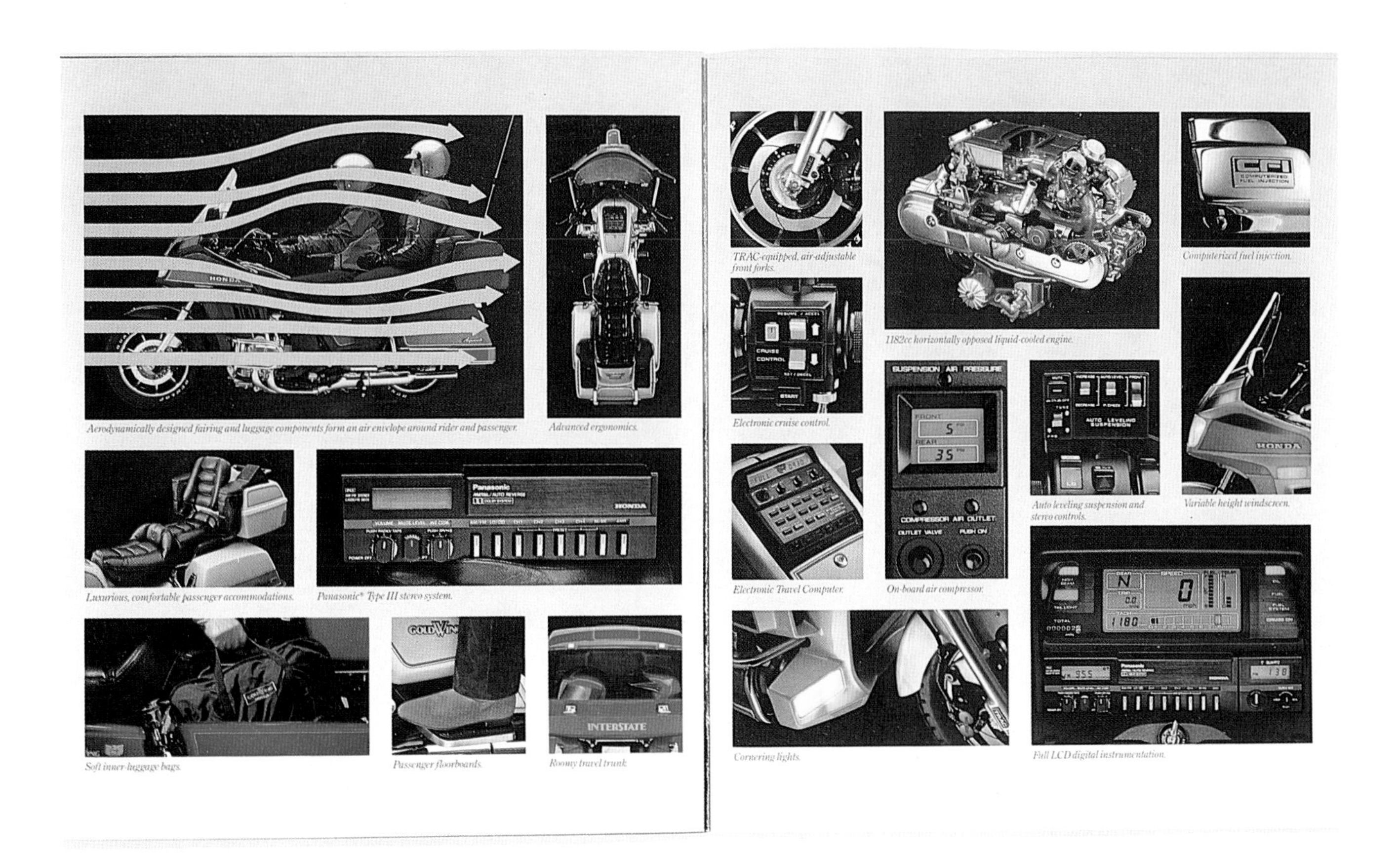

clearance, however, still restricted anyone who foolishly tried to scratch the tourer from corner to corner like King Kenny Roberts.

So what was wrong with the GL1200? Most found the fuel gauge as erratic as earlier versions. After filling the tank to the brim, the gauge didn't move for the first 50 or so miles, then dropped steadily to the half-way mark as another 100 miles were covered. After that, it sank like a stone, hitting the E position while there was still plenty of juice sloshing round inside. As there was no reserve position on the fuel tap, this caused many an anxious moment until the next gas station came into view. Actual fuel consumption on the new Wing varied from 35 mpg when pushed hard to around 45 mpg with lighter throttle loads.

Other gripes? The jumble of wires and cables running down the left handlebar gave a disorganised look, rather out of character with the rest of the neatly finished bike. And finally, the Aspencade's standard sound system, tucked neatly below the instrument cluster, had poor night-time illumination. Yet it still emitted great sounds.

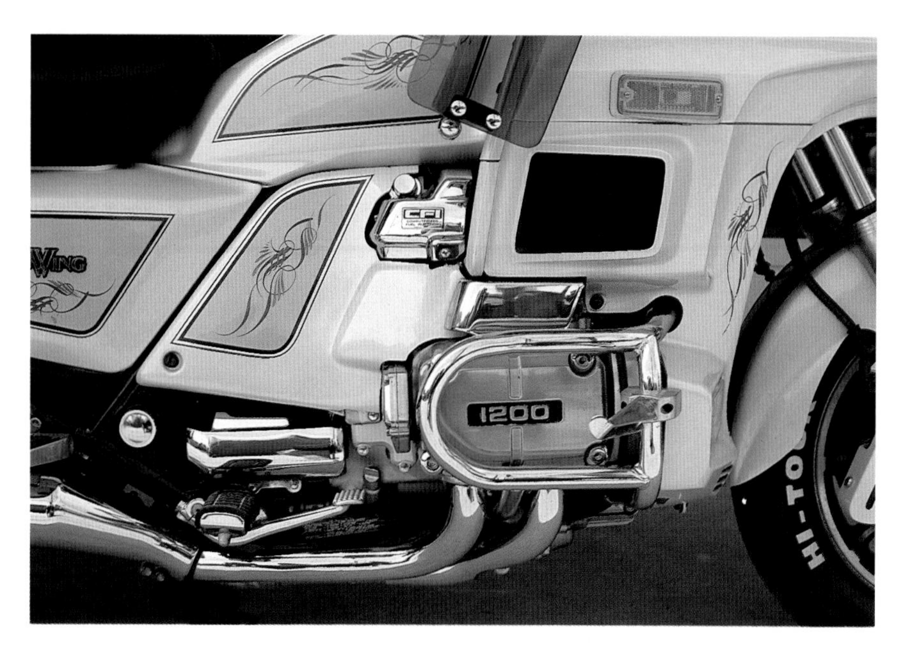

The stereo was made for Honda by Panasonic, and its front panel sported multiple-knobs, dials and LCD readouts; probably of a higher specification than those fitted in many a car. There were eight preset stations, up or down auto scanning, a local/distance switch, a side-load, auto-reverse tape player and an integral intercom. An ambient noise-level adjuster cleverly raised or lowered the stereo's volume depending on the Wing's road speed. So the next time you drew up to a red light, your fellow travellers and the entire neighbourhood did not have to endure a deafening racket.

Small speakers meant bass sounds were weak, but the treble was OK and the Panasonic could be cranked up to produce 105 decibels. Nobody expected seriously good hi-fi on a bike, but Honda's system gave good stereo separation. Some of the buttons were fiddly for gloved hands, but here was the best OEM stereo on a production motorcycle. Interstate owners could buy the same unit from the options list, but it wasn't cheap.

Above
Computerised fuel injection featured on the GL1200 Limited Edition in 1985, and the SE-i a year later. But owners complained of rough running and poor fuel consumption, so the system was dropped for 1987

Right
In its Pearl White livery, the SE-i of 1986 was the most lavishly equipped Gold Wing to date

HONDA
GOLDWING
1200
MICHELIN

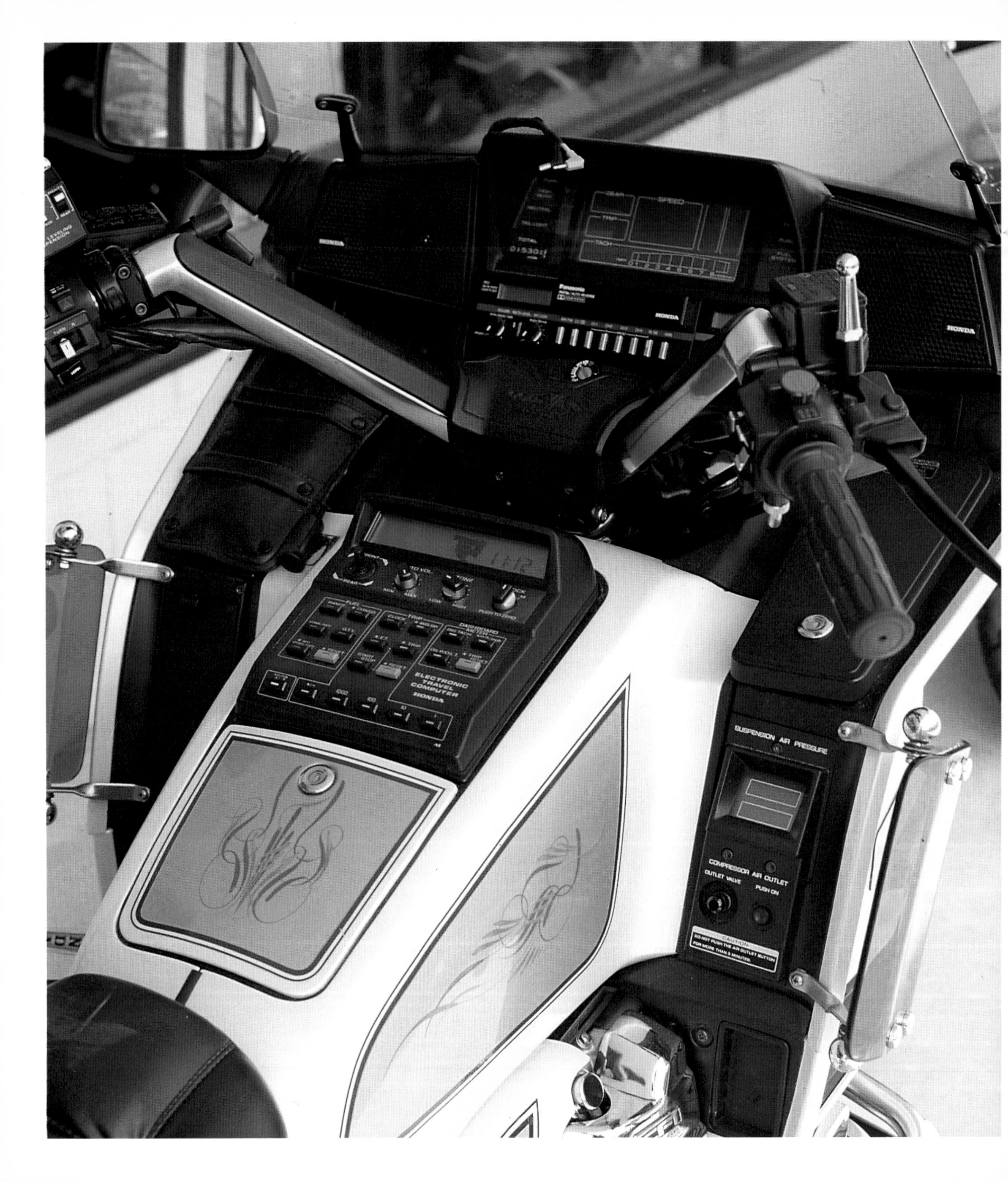
GEAR
SPEED
TRIP
TACH
TOTAL
Panasonic
HONDA
HONDA
HONDA
FUEL
CLOCK
TRIP
DASHBOARD METER
TONE
LOW
HIGH
PUSH TO ZERO
ELECTRONIC
TRAVEL
COMPUTER
HONDA
1000
100
10
SUSPENSION AIR PRESSURE
COMPRESSOR AIR OUTLET
OUTLET VALVE
PUSH ON
CAUTION
DO NOT PUSH THE AIR OUTLET BUTTON
FOR MORE THAN 5 MINUTES.

Above

Cornering lights were included in an extended fairing for the top Aspencades for '85 and '86. The lower part of the fairing also acted as a cover for the conspicuous oil filter cover and water pump everyone had been looking at since 1975

Left

Techno fans could delight in the extraordinary instrumentation of the Aspencade SE-i, which boasted electronic cruise control and even a travel computer. Note also the two-piece handlebars

Thus, 1984 saw a new chapter open in the Wing's illustrious history. American buyers weren't without options when it came to buying a fully-dressed steed – Cavalcades, Ventures and Voyagers were all respectable machines. Once again, however, Honda had raised the stakes, and anyone buying a Japanese-sourced touring motorcycle essentially faced Hobson's Choice.

Leadership of the Gold Wing's development team passed to Hideaki Nebu in 1985. In that same year, Honda finally dropped the unfaired bike from the range, and encountered little protest from any quarter. At the other end of the scale, a new top-of-the-line GL1200 Aspencade Limited Edition was introduced. This version sported fuel injection, cruise control on the handlebar, cornering lights in the fairing lowers, and weighed a lofty 835 lbs fuelled up.

Fuel injection seemed like a good idea in theory, but for once the mighty Honda Motor Company stumbled. Precise fuel delivery by computer monitoring of throttle position, intake vacuum, atmospheric pressure and temperature were promised, but not delivered. Injected bikes were widely accused of rough running and poor performance, caused either by variable fuel quality or the logistics of balancing the mechanical aspects of the system with the precise demands of the controlling computer. The new electronic cruise control device was better received, but the buyers who thought they'd acquired a certain exclusivity when purchasing a Limited Edition were soon in for a shock.

The following model year saw yet another flagship at the head of the range – the Aspencade SE-i. This bike had everything the Limited Edition had trumpeted, and its up-market spec was boosted by auto levelling suspension, a four-speaker radio and a flow-through ventilation system. Installed to combat the partial vacuum that formed behind the fairing, and also prevent the small possibility of exhaust gases being sucked onto this region, this had mixed success. Some air could be felt around the shin area, but the supply from the upper vents was less easy to detect.

Many prospective riders would have been intrigued by yet another new gizmo – an electronic travel computer. With a miniature map of the States at the centre of an LCD strip, this device fed data on fuel range, current and average consumption, plus the amount of fuel consumed and the quantity remaining. It also gave information on trip time, average speed, elapsed time and distance travelled!

Limited Edition owners felt they'd been taken for a ride when the SE-i materialised, and both models proved there was a clear limit to the number of folk prepared to pay a hefty premium for a few fripperies added to the regular Aspencade. Honda doesn't like upsetting its customers, so the 1987 line-up – headed by the 'plain' Aspencade – seemed almost like an act of contrition.

The new bike benefited greatly by its repositioning at the head of the Wing line-up; it included most of the worthwhile improvements of the last two years, jettisoned the fuel injection and other gizmos, and came with an affordable price sticker. Few styling differences could be identified on the bodywork, apart from the blank panels on the fairing lowers to accept auxiliary running lights, and an extension of the fairing into an oil filter cover, just like the Wing's sporty Interceptor stablemate.

Great efforts had been invested in making the '87 GL1200's drivetrain smoother and quieter, via changes to the drive shaft. At its front end this switched from straight-cut bevel gears to a helical type, while the damper spring and take-up cam were also attended to in this area. Other revisions took place on the gear shifter mechanism and clutch friction discs.

These small refinements, when added together, worked wonders for gear selection, which could be commenced without the traditional crunch into first. The rest of the box seemed creamier too. The entire drivetrain now felt less jerky than before, and some of the odd mechanical noises Wing owners had had to put up for over a decade were suddenly silenced. Even the exhaust system was quieter.

Silence was one thing, but comfort was another and, despite numerous changes, the Wing's saddle still had pilots shifting round trying to find a comfortable spot for that ride over the horizon. Honda finally cracked the problem on the 1987 Wings. The new seat was completely reshaped, with wider areas for both rider and passenger, an undercut backrest separating them, and lots of changes to the underlying triple-density foam padding.

In its fourth year of production, Honda had clearly refined the GL1200 Gold Wing about as far as it would go. The latest enhancements, though hardly earth-shattering, were evidence of a constant desire to improve the product and take account of the needs of consumers. The four-cylinder format had been around for a dozen or so years now, and soon Honda was about to confirm its innovative reputation in spectacular fashion.

Above
This badge caused a certain amount of friction when it appeared on the 1986 Aspencade SE-i. The previous year, Aspencade Special Edition owners thought they were getting precisely that, but Honda soon broadened the club. Peace eventually descended in 1987, when the regular Aspencade reverted to the flagship of the range

Right
Aspencade one-upmanship was also on view after dark, as the SE-i featured a signature light in the travel trunk

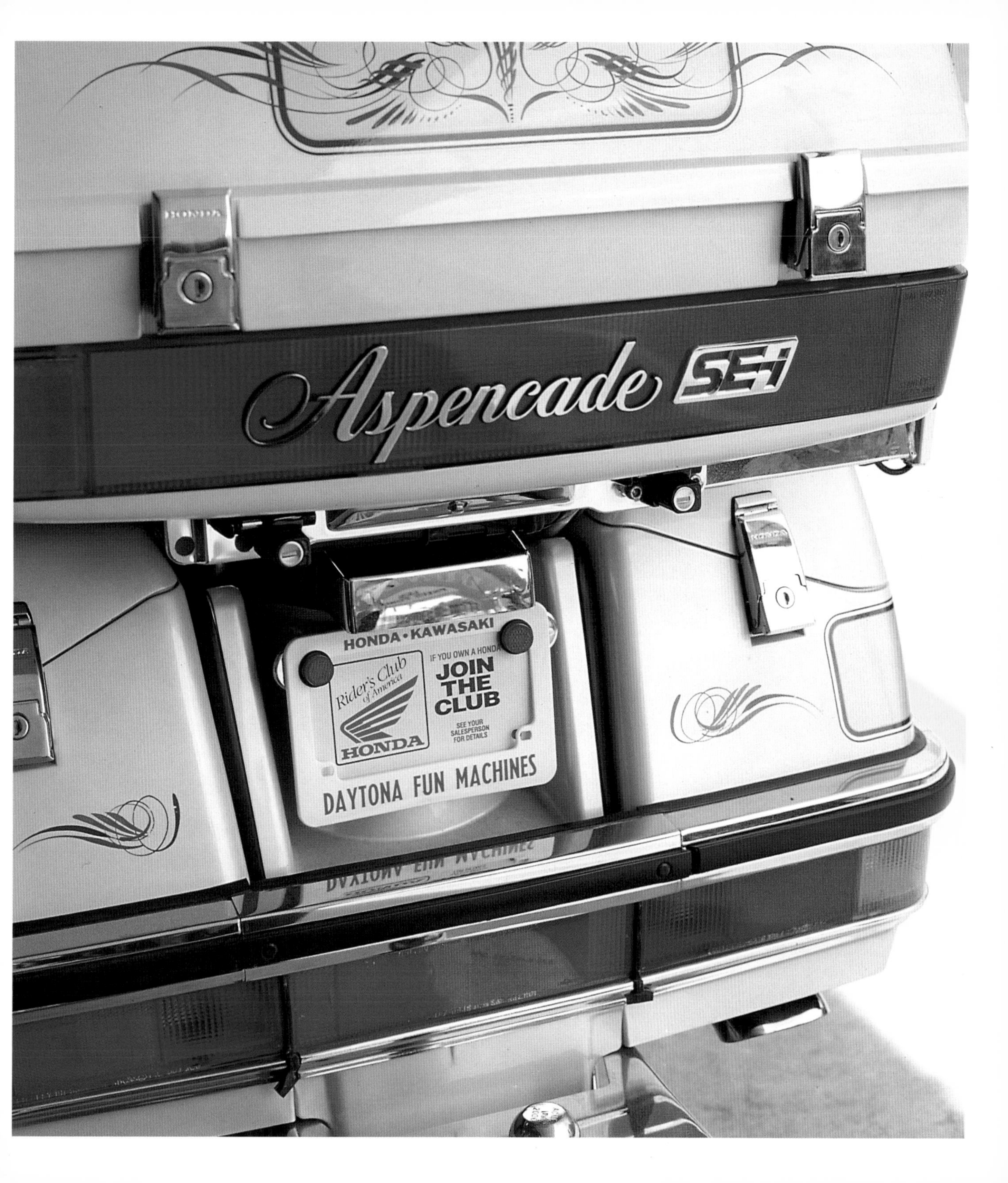
HONDA
Aspencade SEi
HONDA
HONDA • KAWASAKI
Rider's Club of America
HONDA
IF YOU OWN A HONDA
JOIN THE CLUB
SEE YOUR SALESPERSON FOR DETAILS
DAYTONA FUN MACHINES

HONDA

Above

Extending the wheelbase on the 1200 by an extra two inches over the previous model meant the new GL could comfortably accommodate all types and sizes of rider and passenger

Left

Another Wing heads through the countless pines of the Black Hills to home in on Sturgis

Above
The GL1200's straight-line stability gives you plenty of opportunity to gawp at the scenery without wandering around your lane, even when riding with one hand on the bars!

Right
Flying the flag! Few Wings remain standard, but this 1986 Aspencade is one of those rare exceptions

HONDA
GOLDWING
1200

Soaring Higher

As a major producer of cars and motorcycles, the Honda Motor Company has always been aware of the fact that 'new' sells, so they decided it was time the Gold Wing concept was lifted a stage further in its evolution. Previous incarnations of their luxury tourer, like the GL1100 and GL1200, had been created because the competition had got stronger. That wasn't the case in 1988 – now Honda were setting the pace themselves, without reference to anything the rest of the two-wheeled fraternity was up to.

In some ways the wheels of progress turned full circle, because the centrepiece of the all-new GL was a flat-six engine of 1520cc, similar to the six-cylinder 1470cc motor in Honda's AOK prototype of sixteen years earlier. That engine had been deemed too long to give a satisfactory riding position, and a more compact four was adopted for production in 1975. As the '90s approached, Honda ventured further along the high-tech route in their quest to make the GL1500 the definitive two-wheeled tourer.

Whereas the AOK had weighed in at a handy 484 lbs, the new Wing caused gasps of amazement by standing on the scales at a hefty 876 lbs fully fuelled. This figure was mightily close to the outrageous 882 lbs mass of the mid-'80s Kawasaki Voyager 1300cc – a machine that didn't really offer the right sort of dynamic properties. The Honda seemed equally daunting, as its wheelbase had been further eked out to an elongated 66.9 inches, and the machine's overall length was not much short of nine feet!

Further impressive numbers could be plucked out of the hat concerning the new Gold Wing, but not everything was taken to excess. The 1520cc capacity was produced by a sextet of pistons of 71mm bore and 64mm stroke. A capacious 6.3 US (5.3 UK) gallon tank held the fuel delivered by just two 36mm CV carburettors into cylinder heads with a compression ratio of 9.8:1. And the GL1500's gross vehicle weight of 1270 lbs meant a maximum load capacity of 394 lbs. Naturally it had shaft drive, air-adjustable rear suspension and – a Wing first – reverse gear!

Many simply thought the big H had gone over the top this time. With its engine almost totally enclosed, here was yet more ammunition for those who regarded the Wing as nothing more than a two-wheeled car, or

Closer to automotive technology than ever, the GL1500 hit the streets in 1988, just four years after the GL1200 made its debut

GoldWing
GL1500/6

Some European markets like Germany demanded lower windscreen heights and pancake-style travel trunks

luxury limousine. Somewhere, Bill Haylock must have been wearing a wry grin on his face. Yet the six-cylinder machine could also be seen as a logical extension of everything that had gone on since the start of the Gold Wing dynasty in 1975.

Honda's evolution of the Wing had taken a dramatic twist, but the underlying principles were still the same. GL riders, it seemed, wanted an armchair on wheels first and foremost, with comfort and protection from the elements the two key criteria. Speed and handling, though also important, were less critical. So the GL1500's design team spent many hours perfecting the seat and fairing, to cocoon the riders and enable them to travel even further.

Thanks to the huge fairing, which prevented buffeting winds reaching both rider and passenger, protection was almost total. The only glitch came when it rained, as the vast screen was looked through by all but the

The GL1500 may look perfect when complete, but take off that bodywork and frightening things come into view. Because the bike is completely enclosed, some parts never receive attention, or even cleaning, until they break or need replacement. Swapping the rear tyre on a six-pot Wing is not a task to take lightly either

tallest riders (rain may be less common in America, but a wash/wiper system surely wasn't beyond the scope of Honda for its European clientele). Then again, countries like Germany demanded a much lower screen on their imported bikes, sidestepping the problem altogether.

Despite the digital LCD technology of the 1200cc Aspencade's instruments, Honda now reverted to conventional dials with the GL1500. Between the speedometer and tachometer was a rectangular panel displaying the time, radio frequency and, on demand, the suspension pressure. The latter applies only to the rear hybrid unit of the six-cylinder bike, as the front forks were conventional coil-springs with high hydraulic action.

Fuel and temperature gauges at the base of the instrument cluster were surrounded by warning lights for main beam, side stand deployed, low oil and fuel and an illuminated OD to warn that overdrive ratio had been

selected. Inset into the dummy fuel tank was the radio cassette, protected by a removable cover to keep out the weather and any wandering fingers. In other words, plenty of high-tech toys to keep the riders happy.

The original GL1000 was universally regarded as a smooth motorcycle, with the GL1100 and the GL1200 better each time. But the six-cylinder 1520cc unit was clearly the smoothest of the lot. It was like pure liquid gold, with a silky power delivery from low down the rev range through to the paltry 5,500rpm redline. The smooth six gave a feeling of safety and serenity at any speed up to about 110mph – the GL1500's maximum – enabling 600 mile days to be reeled off with impunity.

Honda had long since perfected the on-board compressor for suspension adjustment, so the new Wing handled better on the road than an 876 lb projectile had any right to. Indeed it felt safe and secure at all times, and even quite chuckable – clearly ahead of the smaller, lighter GL1200 in

Above
Neat plate, my friend, if just a little illegal

Right
Three concealed levers at the base of the travel trunk open all three luggage compartments and require just a single lock for better security

GoldWing

GoldWing

scratching terms. Likewise the unified braking system was superb, with large double discs up front and a single disc at the rear, all with twin piston calipers.

In touring mode, fuel consumption averaged 35-40mpg, which wasn't bad for a machine of these proportions. Exploration of the GL1500's full performance dipped the figure somewhere into the mid-20s. That perpetual Achilles Heel of the Wing – the fuel gauge – was once again not noted for its accuracy. A fuel warning light came on after about 170 miles. There was still almost a gallon of fuel left so there was no need to start pushing just yet.

Possibly the only factor that a GL1500 rider had to overcome was the fear of all that weight. Parking lot manoeuvres soon became no problem, especially with the reverse gear if you really got into a spot of bother. A lever by the left shin engaged reverse gear, then by pressing the starter motor button the bike could be shunted slowly but surely backwards. Honda must have done some careful calculations here, as any strain on the

Above
A Pearl White Aspencade SE drifts along the shore at Daytona Beach. During Daytona Bike Week Harley-Davidsons mingle more or less happily with their rivals

Left
An excellent view of the extraordinary cockpit controls of the GL1500. The theory goes that black is very slimming. Probably works for Chanel ballgowns...

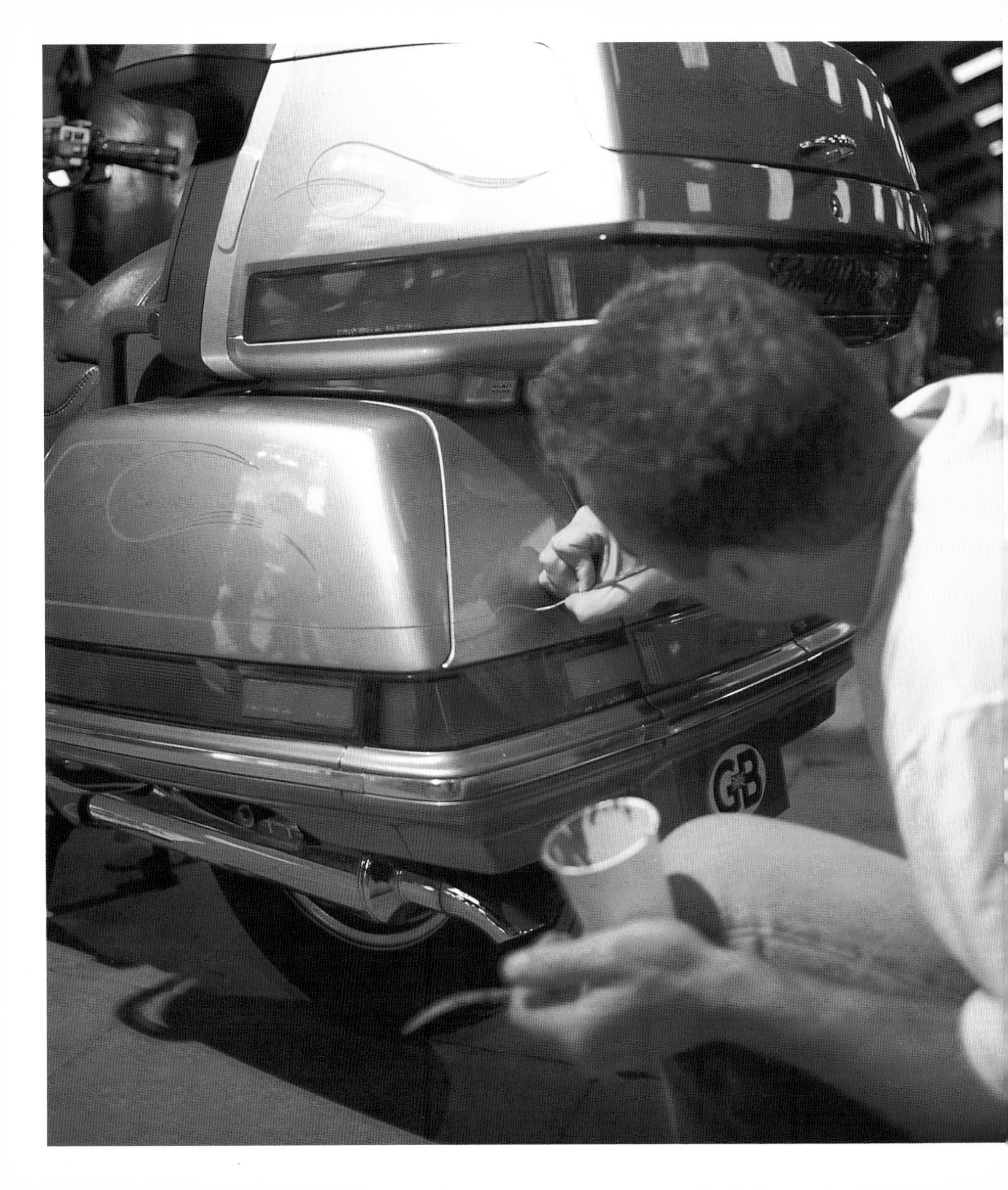

Left
Whatever you do, don't creep up behind this guy and shout "Harley-Davidson Road King!" Custom paint vendors at Wing Dings do a roaring trade in pin-stripes or, indeed, anything that takes your fancy

Above
The wheels of progress epitomised. An early GL1000 with Vetter fairing stands next to a GL1500 – the latest and greatest of the Gold Wing dynasty

starter motor had to be avoided. There was no chance of flattening the battery either, as the engine had to be running for the reverse to operate.

Despite the considerable weight of the GL1500, it proved extremely easy to haul onto its centrestand. I was over in America the year they came out, and a dealer had some fun at my expense. Having owned two 1200s in my time, I was used to grunting the thing onto its stand – no problem, really. But what about an even bigger and heavier machine? The dealer called his daughter over – she was somewhere in her early teens – and asked her to demonstrate for me. It was as easy as pie, and I felt a little sheeping about asking the question.

Though I've never had the misfortune, touch wood, to drop a 1500 yet (or any size Wing for that matter), I've met a few who have. Crashes at higher speeds have often reduced all that shapely plastic bodywork and luggage to scrap, meaning expensive with a capital E. But most shunts

GoldWing
E856
CBU
HONDA
HONDA
GoldWing

occurred at walking pace or, even more embarrassing, at a standstill, when an unwary pilot is caught out by all that weight. Little damage usually results, as the bike just tips over onto its engine protection bars. Only the rider's ego suffers.

The first and second years of GL1500 production were not without their problems. A few gripes about the six-pot's sometimes jerky drivetrain appeared, and from time to time there were other grumbles about the performance of the front forks, brakes, cruise control, windshield adjuster and saddlebag seals. Some isolated clutches and ignition boxes gave up completely. More common was the gearchange's loud clank as you tried to shift smartly from ratio to ratio – a noise made more noticeable by the quietness of the rest of the bike. It was the familiar engine speed/clutch problem, and the key to achieving the occasional perfect noiseless shift was to take things steadily as you moved up through the box. Apart from the gear shifting, all these matters were attended to when the 1990 bikes were wheeled out.

That same year saw the introduction of the SE, or Special Equipment, model. Even more features were added to the basic GL1500. The SE had a weatherproof cover for the seat, adjustable passenger footrests, a stoplight mounted high on the trunk, warm-air lower-leg vents, a vent in the

Left and above

Three wheels are more stable than two, so if the thought of dropping and having to pick up your GL1500 clouds your enjoyment, go for the trike option

windscreen for controlled airflow and illuminated handlebar switches. The extra bits totalled under 10 lbs extra weight, but the price tag climbed substantially over the base model, though part of this was down to the attractive two-tone paint schemes offered.

Honda reinstated the Interstate name to the Gold Wing range, along with the Aspencade, in 1991. The Interstate was the base model, with a lower seat height of 29.5 inches, and it eliminated the reverse gear, cruise control and on-board air compressor features. This reduced weight by 40.4 lbs compared to the Aspencade's 800.4 lbs. All the '91 models were given Anniversary Edition graphics above the Honda nameplate on the front of the fairing and on the dummy tank, to celebrate a decade of US production of the Gold Wing.

At the time of writing, the GL1500 has already enjoyed six years of production life – longer than any previous Wing. Which begs the question, what happens next to Honda's touring legend? The Honda Motor Company is famed for its technical innovation, and has scaled successively higher peaks of engineering virtuosity to transform the two-wheel scene. So will we see a flat-eight cylinder tourer, of even larger capacity?

Many feel the chances are remote. The 1990s have so far seen a holding back as power limits have been reached, or legislated, and in other areas of motorcycling there has been some customer reaction against increasingly high-tech machines. The Gold Wing has already reached what a fighter pilot might regard as the outer limits of its 'performance envelope'. Weight and size specifications are surely at the maximum for a two-wheeler.

Other factors perhaps have more relevance to all this crystal ball-gazing. Unless you've been on a different planet, it won't have escaped your notice that Honda's sporting success has stretched beyond two wheels. The company first won a Formula One GP as far back as 1965, and first held the Formula One championship in 1986 in conjunction with Williams.

This track success helped sales of Honda cars take off, especially in America. Their modern range of cars are as far away from the first model – 1962's S360 – as the GL1500SE is from the 50cc two-stroke that started the ball rolling. In the 1990s, the Accord model outsold Ford and GM on their home ground – an astonishing achievement. In many ways, the car division is way ahead, and leads to some sobering facts facing Wing nuts. Currently just 10% of Honda's production capacity is devoted to two-wheelers, and the whole motorcycle division generates a measly 1% of the company's profits! Suddenly two-wheelers look like small fry in a rather large stretch of water.

Even though the West is far from reaching saturation point, it is interesting to observe Honda's policy of moving into Third World countries to maintain its expansion. Trade barriers and red tape tend to

Above
Wings and other machines congregate under the gaze of presidents at Mount Rushmore in South Dakota – one of the many neighbouring attractions for rallygoers at nearby Sturgis

Right
That wide and tall fairing gives a rider unsurpassed protection from the elements. You have to be unusually tall to stand any chance of looking over the screen

Touring choice boils down to just two types of motorcycles for most Americans. On the one hand there's the traditional approach, personified by the Harley-Davidson Electra Glide and Tour Glide. Or there's the high-tech route, exemplified by Honda's six-cylinder GL1500. The two machines perform similar functions but could hardly be more polarised

miraculously dissolve when the big H unleashes promises of overseas investment and employment for job-hungry markets. This enables the company to cash in on the more modest demands of these nations, and offload basic, low-tech models that simply wouldn't succeed in the more sophisticated marketplaces of Europe and the Americas.

Sadly, Soichiro Honda died in 1991, but not before realising his ambition to transform the way the world perceives the motorcycle. His successors will probably ensure Honda remains a major player in the motorcycle market for the foreseeable future. What form that will take, however, only a few are privy to.

On one occasion Soichiro Honda explained that his company did not respond to market forces: "We create demand." The Gold Wing in its latest guise is a prime example of this philosophy. There was no obvious demand for such a leviathan, yet it sells.

When you see a custom-painted GL1000 on the tank, you know that here's a GL1500 owner with a clear sense of Wing history

However, politics and marketing strategies are beyond the scope of a book like this. We're here to celebrate a motorcycle, not worry about what it might become. The Honda Gold Wing has no equal in the wide open spaces of the USA, nor in the narrower routes of Europe. This Honda two-wheeler may embody several car-type principles, but when it makes touring this good, who cares?

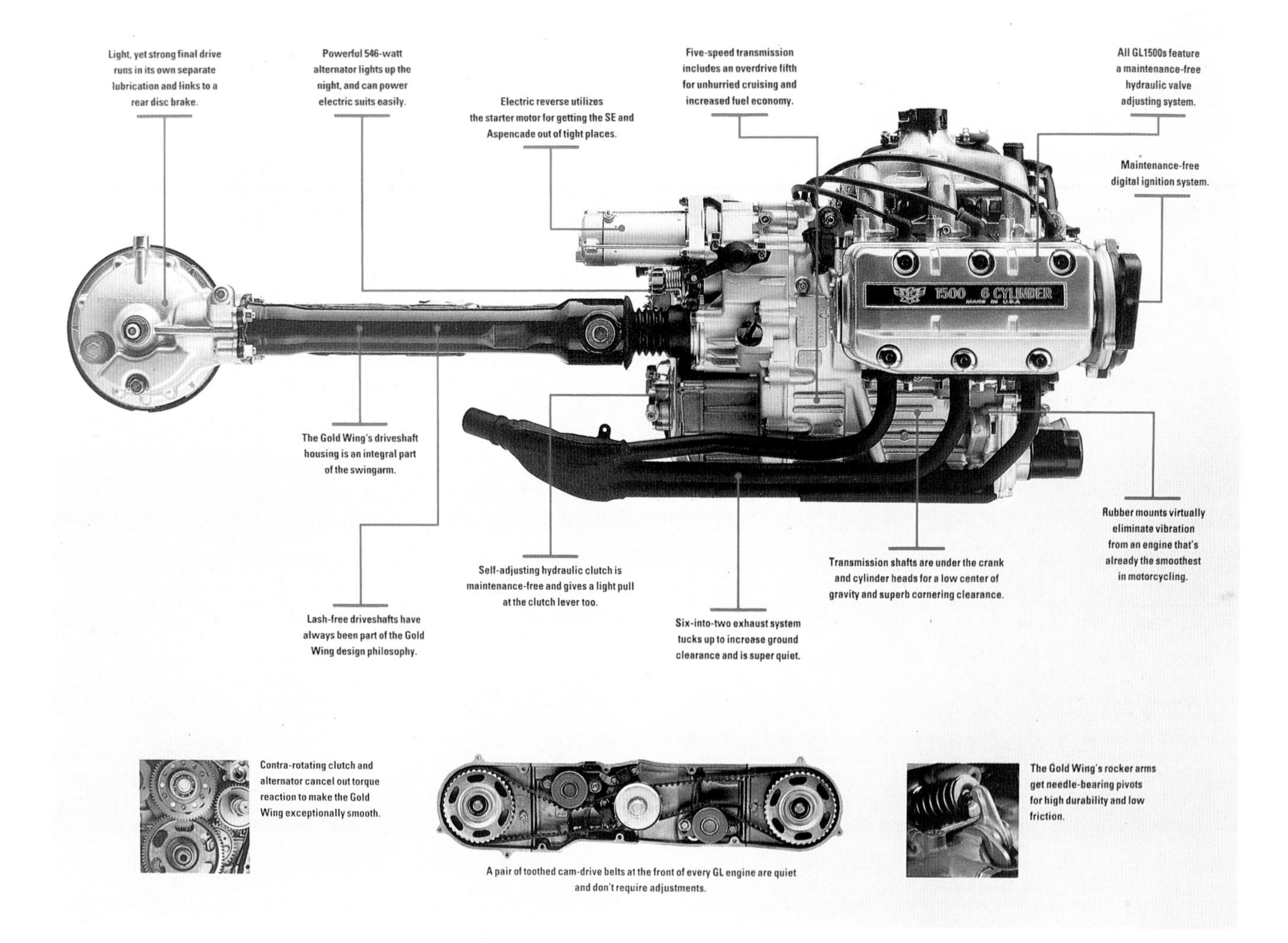

Above

Honda's latest publicity material for the GL1500 emphasises the traditional durability and reliability of the horizontally opposed engine and shaft drive unit. Maintenance-free electronic and mechanical details promise countless thousands of miles of motoring before the six has to be torn down

Right

For some owners even the extraordinarily well-equipped Aspencade SE still isn't enough. This guy has piled yet more gold onto his golden Gold Wing

HONDA
TEMP
AIR PRESSURE CONTROL
P.CHECK
INCREASE
OUTLET
DECREASE
GoldWing

Above

A GL1100 K3 fitted with Vetter touring accessories shows just how far the GL1500s parked alongside have taken fairing and luggage integration

Opposite and overleaf

Everyone is allowed to dream, and this GL1500 owner from the plains of Iowa clearly thinks freedom is a log cabin high up in some wilderness retreat. Though it's got plenty of ground clearance, I'd still like to watch him wrestle the big Wing up that mountain trail!

Gold Wing
WB7231
NOV
93

GoldWing
WB7231
NOV
93

If you're going to transfer a scene onto those big areas of fibreglass, you might as well let your imagination run riot; or in this case, get a kickstart from Salvador Dali. The title of the original painting is Dream caused by the flight of a bee around a pomegranate one second before waking up. *Whatever Salvador was on, it wasn't a Gold Wing: the painting dates from 1944. This GL1500 SE and sidecar always draws lots of admiring glances*

BIKE

Above

Even greater enclosure of the engine is afforded by the GL1500, as this side-by-side shot with a 1200 reveals. The continuity of styling themes can also be appreciated

Left

GL1500 in its logical colour. 86 lb heavier than the 1200, and an incredible 226 lb more than the GL1000, just about enough extra metal to strip down and make up a Honda Cub!

Above
The GL1500's l-o-n-g 66.9 inch wheelbase is obvious in this shot, as is the low 30 inch seat height. A motorcycle you sit in, not on

Left
Makes a change from the customary eagle!

Above
The rakish front of the six-cylinder and that enclosed front-end make it a perfect canvas for personalised statements. Deep blue paint is a great foil for all that gleaming chrome

Left
Sophisticated electronic cruise control on the GL1500 sticks like a leech to your selected speed, varying by about 1 mph only, regardless of gradient. It can also be adjusted up or down a touch while the bike is still rolling

Overleaf
Supreme rider comfort, here augmented by a backrest, is yours with a GL1500

GL 1500/6

HONDA
GL 1500/6

Left
Flick up the side-stand and away you go. The GL1500 will take you round the block or across a continent

Above
Despite weighing around 1000 lbs fully-laden, and with occupants aboard, six-pot power still delivers almost rocket-like acceleration up to 100mph

A six-into-two exhaust system is tucked under the 1520cc motor, but some owners still like to remind those in their trail that there are a lot of cylinders underneath that throttle

SE models feature an adjustable vent in the windshield to allow some cooling air to reach the riders and relieve the pressure that can build up behind them

If you wish to pose, the GL1500 motor is tractable enough to lope along the beach at walking pace

CX 1186
FLOYD

HONDA
HONDA
GL 1500/6

Above left
When the 1500's vast luggage capacity can't hold everything you want to tote, hitch up a colour-matched trailer

Left
An early Honda promotional shot of the GL1500 shows how plastic panels hide the complex workings to give a clean and tidy look to the bodywork

Above
Despite being the heaviest and bulkiest of the Wings, the 1500 is also the most willing in corners and exhibits surprising scratchability

Above
A machine fit to grace any cafe society

Above right
After the high-tech LCD instruments of the 1100 and 1200 Aspencades, the GL1500 reverted to simpler analogue dials. A digital panel between the speedometer and tachometer displays the time, radio wavelength and, on demand, the suspension air pressure. There is also a cluster of warning lights below

Right
On this GL1500 rocker box cover it says 'Made in USA'. Since 1980, the Gold Wing has been built in its principal North American market, at the Marysville, Ohio plant

mph
km/h
4:25
x1000min
SIDE STAND

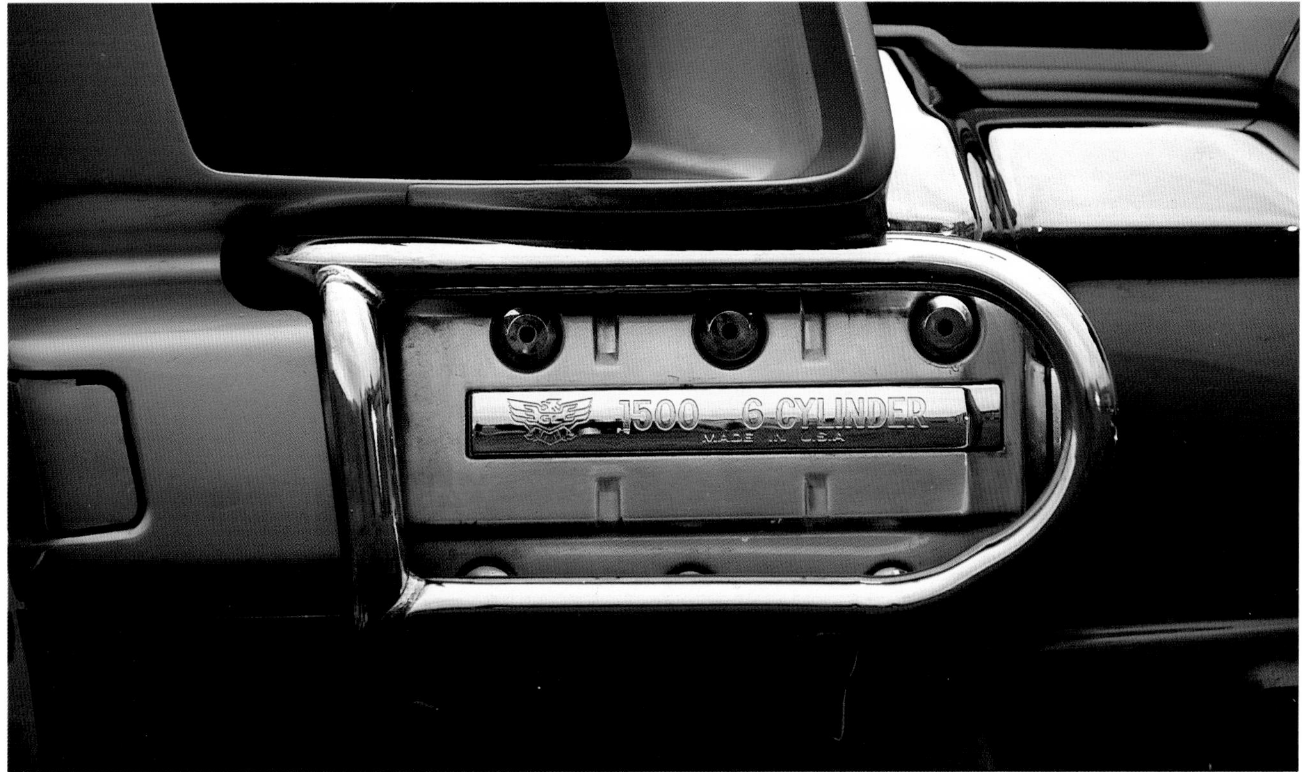
1500 6 CYLINDER
MADE IN U.S.A

Honda Gold Wing Specifications

1975 GL1000

ENGINE: Water-cooled OHC flat four
CAPACITY: 999cc
BORE & STROKE: 72mm x 61.4mm
COMPRESSION RATIO: 9.2:1
POWER: 78 bhp
MAXIMUM REVS: 8500rpm
CARBURATION: 4 x 32mm CV
IGNITION: Coil and contact breaker
TRANSMISSION: Five speed, shaft final drive
SUSPENSION: Front and rear – coil spring/hydraulic
BRAKES: Front – twin discs, single piston caliper; rear – single disc, single piston caliper
TYRES: FRONT – 3.50 X 19; REAR – 4.50 X 17
FUEL CAPACITY: 19 litres
WHEELBASE: 60.5 inches
WEIGHT: 650 lbs (wet)

1980 GL1100 Interstate

ENGINE: WATER-COOLED OHC FLAT FOUR
CAPACITY: 1085cc
BORE & STROKE: 75mm x 61.4mm
COMPRESSION RATIO: 9.2:1
POWER: 81 bhp
MAXIMUM REVS: 8000rpm
CARBURATION: 4 x 30mm CV
IGNITION: Electronic
TRANSMISSION: Five speed, shaft final drive
SUSPENSION: Front – air/coil spring; rear – air/oil
BRAKES: Front – twin discs, single piston caliper; rear – single disc, single piston caliper
TYRES: Front – 110/90-19; rear – 130/90-17
FUEL CAPACITY: 20 litres
WHEELBASE: 63.2 inches
WEIGHT: 748 lbs (wet)

1984 GL1200 Aspencade

ENGINE: Water-cooled OHC flat four
CAPACITY: 1182cc
BORE & STROKE: 75.5mm x 66mm
COMPRESSION RATIO: 9:1
POWER: 94 bhp
MAXIMUM REVS: 7500rpm
CARBURATION: 4 x 32mm CV
IGNITION: Electronic
TRANSMISSION: Four speed plus overdrive, shaft final drive
SUSPENSION: Front – air-adjustable with anti-dive; rear – air/hydraulic
BRAKES: Front – twin discs, twin piston calipers; rear – single disc, twin piston calipers
TYRES: Front – 130/90-16; rear – 150/90-15
FUEL CAPACITY: 22 litres
WHEELBASE: 63.4 inches
WEIGHT: 790 lbs (wet)

1988 GL1500

ENGINE: Water-cooled OHC flat six
CAPACITY: 1520cc
BORE & STROKE: 71mm x 64mm
COMPRESSION RATIO: 9.8:1
POWER: 100 bhp
MAXIMUM REVS: 5500rpm
CARBURATION: 2 x 36mm CV
IGNITION: Electronic
TRANSMISSION: Four speed plus overdrive, shaft final drive
SUSPENSION: Front – coil spring/hydraulic; rear – air-assisted hybrid
BRAKES: Front – dual disc, twin piston calipers; rear – single disc, twin-piston caliper
TYRES: Front – 130/70-18; rear – 160/80-16
FUEL CAPACITY: 24 litres
WHEELBASE: 66.9 inches
WEIGHT: 876 lbs (wet)

Gold Wing Organizations

Gold Wing owners love to get together – indeed, Honda's tourer has easily the largest following for a single model of motorcycle in the whole world. There are clubs and rallies all over America, Britain and the rest of Europe. The smaller meetings – Wing Dings – are usually enjoyable weekend camps for anything from 100 to 300 riders and their bikes, all GLs of course. A bigger international meeting involving thousands of people is called a Treffen – the German word for a gathering of friends. There are well over 100,000 members of Gold Wing clubs worldwide, with more than 3000 in Britain. The Wing is a democratic sort of bike, and its non-aggressive image attracts owners varying in age from 18 to 80. They come from all kinds of backgrounds too. It was interesting to find out the breakdown of machinery in the Gold Wing Owners' Club Of Great Britain which, according to their latest figures, worked out as follows:

GL1500 36%
GL1200 29%
GL1100 23%
GL1000 9%
sidecar outfits 3%

Here are the contact addresses of the major clubs in the UK and USA:

Gold Wing Owners' Club of Great Britain
c/o Dave Horner,
Secretary, GWOCGB,
18 Arncliffe Way,
Cottingham,
North Humberside. HU16 5DH
Tel: (0482) 847307

Gold Wing Road Riders' Association
PO Box 14350,
Phoenix,
Arizona 85063.
Tel: (602) 269 1403